Model Essays for IB and A Level Economics

MACROECONOMICS Volume 2

Kelvin Hong

Ang Jun Yang

First Printing: 2020

ISBN 978-981-14-5054-9

Edventures Pte Ltd

Singapore

www.TheEconomicsTutor.com

Acknowledgments

This work would not have been possible without the help of Jade Chan who helped in drafting and editing the work.

PREFACE

This book answers 20 key examination questions across the entire Macroeconomics syllabus and was created to provide students with the ability to excel in their examinations.

Very often, students are unable to provide step-by-step explanations and relevant evaluation points, which are essential to scoring in examinations.

By studying through the model essays provided in this book, students will also be able to better understand the various economic concepts covered in the Macroeconomics syllabus. The powerful diagrammatic analyses provided will also train students to illustrate economic concepts logically, and enable them to use such diagrams for analyses in a more effective and concise manner.

The questions are mostly obtained from past IB examination papers. However, they are also very applicable to the A Level examinations.

We hope students will now see great hope in scoring very well for their essay papers.

Kelvin Hong & Ang Jun Yang

Table of Contents

1. Explain how a producer price index could be useful in predicting future inflation. (10)

Introduction

1. Inflation is a sustained increase in the general price levels (GPL) of an economy over time.

2. Inflation can be measured using the consumer price index (CPI), which tracks the change in prices of a basket of goods and services consumed by the average household.

3. The Producer Price Index (PPI), on the other hand, measures the average change over time in the selling prices received by domestic producers for their output.

CPI and PPI

1. The PPI is similar to the CPI in that it tracks changes in price, relative to the price in a given base year which is chosen with an index value of 100.

2. Furthermore, similar to the CPI, the PPI is based on a weighted average, where the weights are determined by the relative importance of the components in terms of their share of total national output.

3. However, the PPI looks at rising prices from the perspective of the producer rather than the consumer.

4. While the CPI looks at final prices paid by consumers, the PPI takes a step back and determines the change in the output prices borne by producers at various stages of the production process.

Detailed explanation of PPI

1. There is the PPI for raw inputs, namely raw materials like iron ore and wheat. There is a PPI for intermediate goods, such as refined sugars and leather. Finally, a PPI for final goods at wholesale but not retail level (namely, the price producers directly receive, and not the price consumers pay).

2. When firms experience higher input costs, these costs are ultimately passed on to consumers. For example, if prices of inputs or intermediate prices are rising, it is likely that the prices consumers pay for the final goods will rise at a later date. Likewise, if wholesale prices are rising, it also suggests that the higher prices will eventually be passed on to consumers.

3. For example, should there be an increase in the cost of cows, consumers will eventually have to pay more for handbags made from cow leather. This is because, as cows (the raw input) become more expensive, it costs more to produce leather (the intermediate good), and these costs are eventually transferred on to the handbag (final product). The handbag-producing firm, facing increasing costs of production, would want to charge a higher price, causing the wholesale price to increase. Soon, this translates to increased retail costs of handbags borne by consumers.

4. Economists can thus forecast the future movement of the finished goods PPI by monitoring the intermediate PPI, and the direction of the intermediate PPI can be determined by analysing the inputs PPI.

5. In turn, the rate of inflation can be accurately predicted ahead of time, by tracking the PPI at its various stages.

2. Using the Keynesian AD/AS diagram, explain why an economy may be in equilibrium at any level of real output. (10)

Introduction

1. A macroeconomic equilibrium refers to the state of the economy where there is no tendency towards a contraction or expansion. This occurs when the economy is producing a level of real output corresponding to the intersection of Aggregate Demand (AD) and Aggregate Supply (AS).

2. Aggregate Demand (AD) refers to the total quantity of final goods and services that all buyers in an economy (consumers, firms, the government and foreigners) want to buy over a particular time period, at different possible price levels, ceteris paribus.

3. Aggregate Supply (AS) refers to the total quantity of final goods and services that would be produced in an economy over a particular time period, at different price levels, ceteris paribus.

4. Real Output is measured in terms of Real Gross Domestic Product (RGDP), the total value of all final goods and services produced within the geographical boundaries of an economy over a given time period, after being adjusted for price changes.

Explanation

1. Keynesian economic theory holds that the economy is unable to move into the "long-run", as factor prices and wages will remain inflexible, especially downwards. Reasons include trade union resistance, minimum wage laws, and fixed wage contracts that prevent downward adjustments to wages.

2. Consequently, unlike Classical economic theory, deflationary and inflationary gaps are persistent and not self-correcting.

3. Therefore, the economy may be at equilibrium at any level of real output, and not only at the full-employment output level Y_{fe}, where all resources within the economy are utilised efficiently.

Diagrammatic Explanation

1. This is illustrated through the three sections of the Keynesian AS curve – the horizontal, upward-sloping and vertical sections. Depending on the level of AD in the economy, equilibrium positions can be found on any section of the curve.

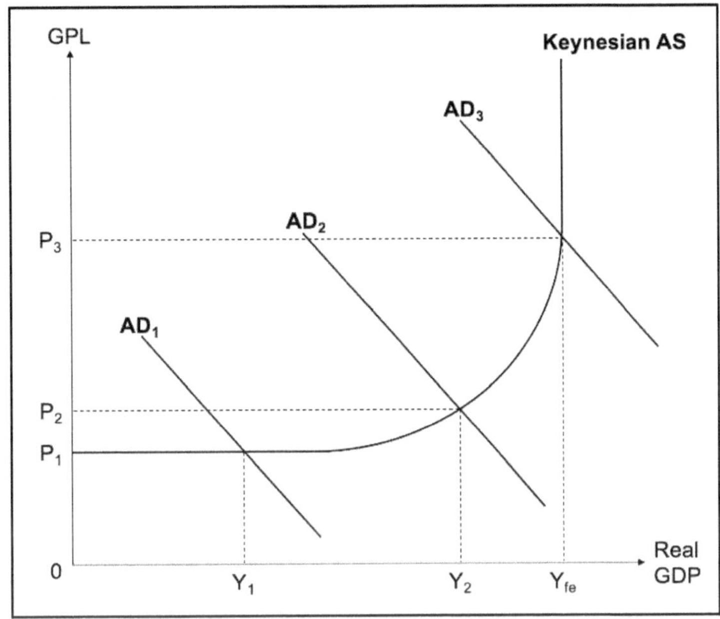

Fig. 1. The three sections of the Keynesian AS curve.

2. For example, following the onset of the Great Depression in the 1930s, which caused a persistently pessimistic economic outlook, consumer and investment expenditure fell. This led to low levels of AD in the US economy, best represented by the curve AD_1, along the horizontal section of the Keynesian AS curve – where there is massive unemployment of resources and high spare capacity (unused factor inputs). Despite this, wages remained quite fixed due to the combination of the above-mentioned reasons. Thus, there is no reduction in unit costs and increase in output that would gravitate the economy towards Y_{fe}. At Y_1, the economy is already at equilibrium.

3. AD_2 is a reflection of the current state of the US economy in 2018, which enjoys modest levels of economic growth. Consequently, the economy operates along the upward-sloping segment of the AS curve, where most resources are already utilised and hence there is limited spare capacity available. Resource prices are bid up by firms seeking to increase their production, causing an increase in the General Price Level (GPL). The economy attains an equilibrium output level at Y_2.

4. AD_3 reflects an economy operating along the vertical segment of the Keynesian AS curve, indicating that all resources available in the economy are already being fully employed. The economy is producing at its full employment level of output, Y_{fe} – this represents the equilibrium real output of the economy.

3. Using the concept of the Keynesian multiplier, explain the possible impact of a rise in government spending on economic growth. (10)

Introduction

1. Economic growth refers to the increase in the value of final goods and services produced by an economy over a period of time. Economic growth encompasses both actual and potential economic growth.

2. Actual growth is the annual percentage increase in the real GDP or output of an economy. This comes about through an increase in the Aggregate Demand (AD) and/or Short-run Aggregate Supply (SRAS).

3. Potential growth refers to the rate at which the economy could grow at if all resources were efficiently employed. It comes about through an expansion of the productive capacity of the economy, leading to an increase in the Long-run Aggregate Supply (LRAS).

Explanation of the Keynesian multiplier

1. An autonomous rise in Government spending (G) leads to an unplanned rundown of inventories by firms.

2. This leads to profit-maximising firms increasing production, thus increasing their derived demand for factors of production. This leads to increased payment of factor income to households.

3. The increased income causes a round of induced consumption, which triggers another round of increased production which will lead to a further increase in income and induced consumption.

4. This is the Keynesian multiplier process at work, which occurs based on the fundamental principle that one person's spending is another's income, leading to multiple rounds of spending and income generation.

5. The multiplier process can be illustrated diagrammatically by successive increases in AD, starting from AD_1, as seen in Fig. 2 on the next page.

6. Overall, Aggregate Demand has risen from AD_1 to AD_5, with the dotted lines representing each round of the multiplier effect.

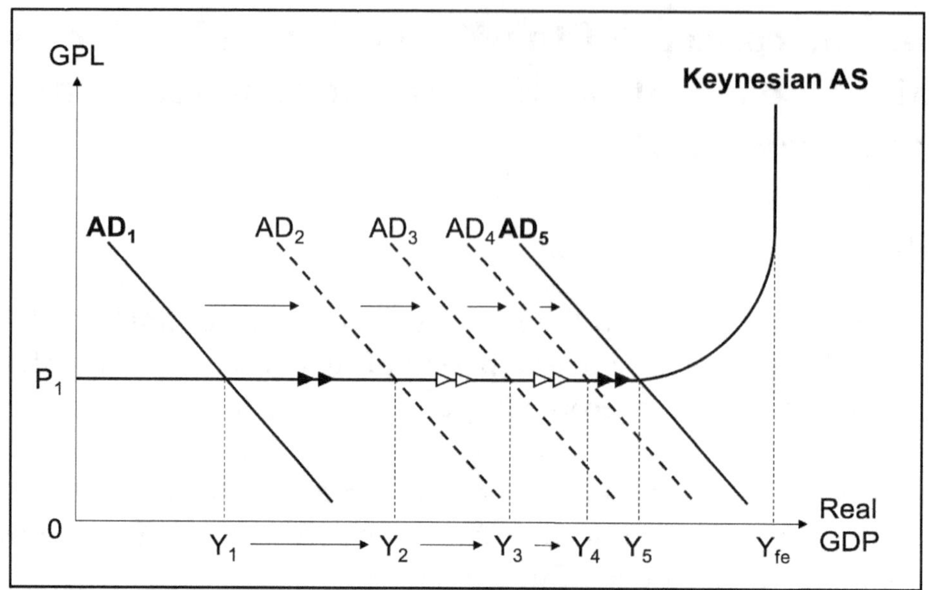

Fig. 2. The Multiplier Effect leading to successive increases in AD.

7. As seen above, an initial government spending of Y_1Y_2 has resulted in an increase in real GDP by Y_1Y_2, but through an increase in induced consumption, there are successive rounds of increase in AD causing to real GDP to ultimately increase to Y_5. Thus, the multiplier process has led to an increase in RGDP that is greater than the initial increase in G, via the formula —

$$\Delta RGDP = k(\Delta AE)$$

8. Where AE is Aggregate expenditure.

9. This continues until all the increase in Government spending as been leaked out of the circular flow of income in the form of Savings, Taxes and Import Expenditure.

10. The size of the multiplier (k) is determined by the marginal propensity to save (MPS), tax (MPT) and import (MPM), by the formula :

$$k = \frac{1}{MPM + MPS + MPT}$$

Or

$$k = \frac{1}{MPW}$$

11. Where marginal propensity to withdraw (MPW) = MPM+MPS+MPT.

12. The smaller the MPW, the larger the size of k, and the greater the impact of an increase in G on Economic Growth.

13. The above analysis assumes that there is adequate spare capacity in the economy to accommodate the full multiplier process.

14. Assuming an MPW value of 0.4, the size of k would be 1 ÷ 0.4 = 2.5. Hence, an increase in G by $ 10 million would lead to a rise in RNY by $ 25 million. Thus, a rise in government spending will lead to a more than proportionate increase in Real GDP.

4. Explain two factors which might cause economic growth. (10)

Introduction

1. Economic growth refers to the increase in the value of final goods and services produced by an economy over a period of time. It consists of actual and potential economic growth.

2. Actual growth is the annual percentage increase in the real GDP or output of an economy. This comes about through an increase in the Aggregate Demand (AD) and / or Short-run Aggregate Supply (SRAS).

3. Potential growth refers to the rate at which the economy could grow at if all resources were efficiently employed. It comes about through an expansion of the productive capacity of the economy, leading to an increase in the Long-run Aggregate Supply (LRAS).

Actual Economic Growth

1. An increase in any of the components of the AD, ceteris paribus, could result in actual economic growth.

2. For example, in 2017, the Chinese government implemented an infrastructure project to the tune of 2.12 trillion yuan ($ 323 billion).

3. The extent and swiftness of this increase in government expenditure (G), a component of AD, was sufficient enough to cause a marked increase in the AD.

4. Diagrammatically, this is seen in Fig. 3 as an increase in Aggregate Demand from AD to AD', which creates a shortage at the original price level P that places an upward pressure on the general price level towards P'. Consequently, firms increase their production to meet this increased demand, resulting in a greater real output (GDP) produced in the economy, from Y to Y'.

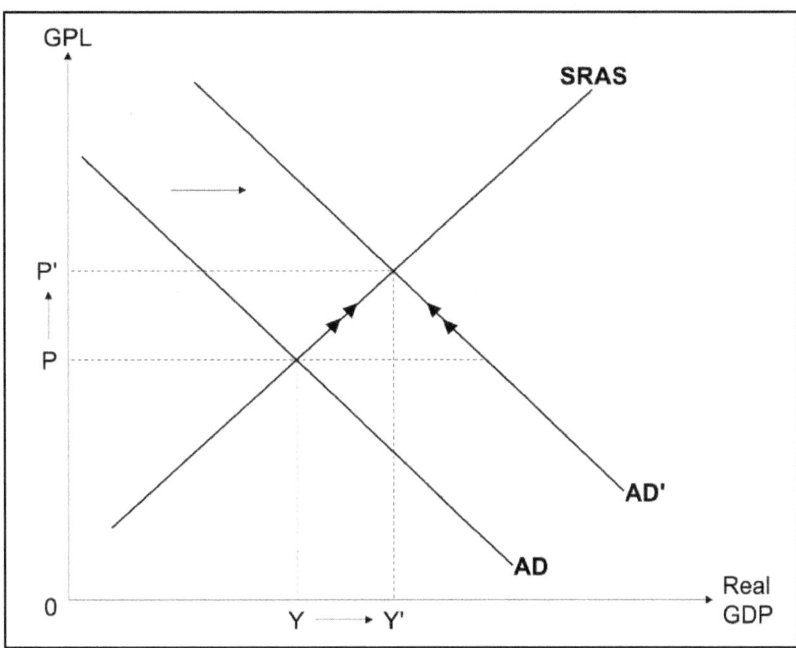

Fig. 3. An Increase in AD leading to Actual Growth.

Potential Economic Growth

1. The Chinese government's infrastructure spending could also lead to potential economic growth. The project involved building over 5,000 kilometres of new expressways, and renovating/repairing 216,000 kilometres of existing roads. This increases the quantity and quality of China's transport infrastructure. As a result, this would increase productivity, expand the productivity capacity, and cause LRAS to increase to LRAS' as seen in Fig. 4 on the next page. This creates an increase in the potential output of the economy, from Y_{fe} to Y_{fe}', implying that potential growth has occurred.

2. Such a project will also likely result in an increase in the SRAS as seen in Fig 4, due to the increased productivity translating to lower unit costs of production for firms, leading to actual growth as well.

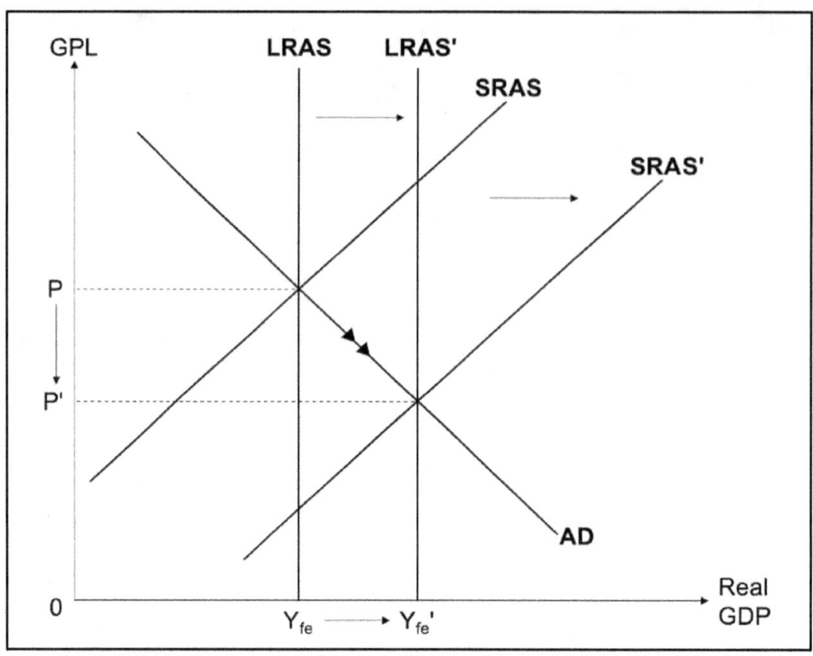

Fig. 4. An Increase in LRAS and SRAS leading to Potential and Actual Growth.

5. Using an appropriate diagram, explain how a recession might lead to more poverty. (10)

Introduction

1. A recession refers to two or more consecutive quarters of negative economic growth (falling real GDP).

2. Real gross domestic product (GDP) refers to the total value of all final goods and services produced within the geographical boundaries of an economy over a given period of time, typically a year, after removing the effects of price changes.

3. Poverty refers to the inability of an individual or family to afford an adequate standard of goods and services. This definition encompasses absolute and relative poverty.

4. Absolute poverty is defined in relation to a nationally or internationally determined 'poverty line', which determines the minimum income that can sustain a family in terms of its basic needs. The World Bank defines the International Poverty Line as living on US$ 1.90 or less a day, per individual.

5. On the other hand, relative poverty is defined in relation to what is 'typical' or average in a given society. As incomes in the society increase, this typical standard also rises.

Explanation

1. A recession can occur due to decreasing Aggregate Demand (AD) in the economy.

2. For example, in the 2008 Great Recession, falling confidence led to decreased consumer (C) and investment (I) expenditures, both of which are components of AD.

3. This caused a decrease in AD, diagrammatically represented by a leftward shift of the AD curve in Fig. 5 from AD to AD'.

4. The decrease in AD creates a surplus at the original General Price Level (GPL), placing a downward pressure on the price level. This reduced profit margins, disincentivising firms from producing, causing a decrease in the real output of the economy from Y to Y'.

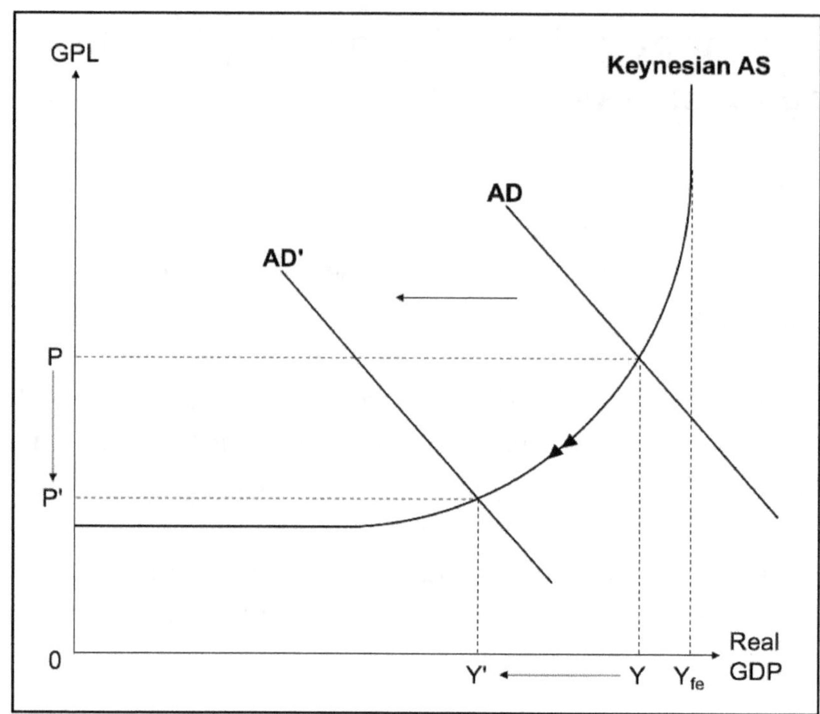

Fig. 5. A decrease in AD resulting in increased Poverty.

5. This translates to a decrease in the real GDP per capita of the economy (assuming a constant population size). The average person in the economy will now receive a lower income and some may be retrenched as demand for workers fall due to lesser output produced.

6. As purchasing power is lowered, people may be brought into relative poverty, as they are unable to purchase as many goods and services as what is deemed typical in the society. For example, some may now have to forego eating out at shopping malls.

7. Additionally, if the recession is severe enough, this may cause those in the economy who were already poor to be forced to live off less than US$ 1.90 a day, plunging them into absolute poverty. This is especially so for those who are retrenched, and who now only have the opportunity of odd jobs.

6. Explain how an increase in investment might affect aggregate demand and aggregate supply. (10)

Introduction

1. Investment refers to spending by firms or the government on new capital goods (i.e. factories, machinery, equipment) and all spending on new construction (housing and other buildings).

2. Aggregate Demand (AD) refers to the total quantity of final goods and services that all buyers in an economy (consumers, firms, the government and foreigners) want to buy over a particular time period, at different possible price levels, ceteris paribus.

3. Aggregate Supply (AS) refers to the total quantity of final goods and services that would be produced in an economy over a particular time period, at different price levels, ceteris paribus.

Explanation

1. For example, in 2016 the Multi-National Corporation (MNC) Micron announced plans to invest US$ 4 billion to expand its factories in Singapore. Such investment activities involve spending on capital goods, namely machinery and equipment used in manufacturing processes. This constitutes a specific form of investment, known as Foreign Direct Investment.

2. This would lead to an increase in the Investment expenditure (I), a component of AD. Consequently, AD will increase. Referring to Fig. 6 on the next page, AD increases from AD_1 to AD_2.

3. Simultaneously, this increased spending on capital goods would increase the number of machines and equipment, leading to an increase in the quantity of Factors of Production (FOPs). Furthermore, new capital goods would likely involve more advanced technology, thus the quality of capital is improved as well.

4. Hence, productive capacity expands, leading to an increase in the Long-Run part of AS. With more capital goods, productivity may increase, and may lead to a fall in the unit cost of production, leading to an increase in the Short-Run part of the AS as well.

5. Overall, Keynesian AS increases from AS_1 to AS_2 as seen in Fig. 6 below.

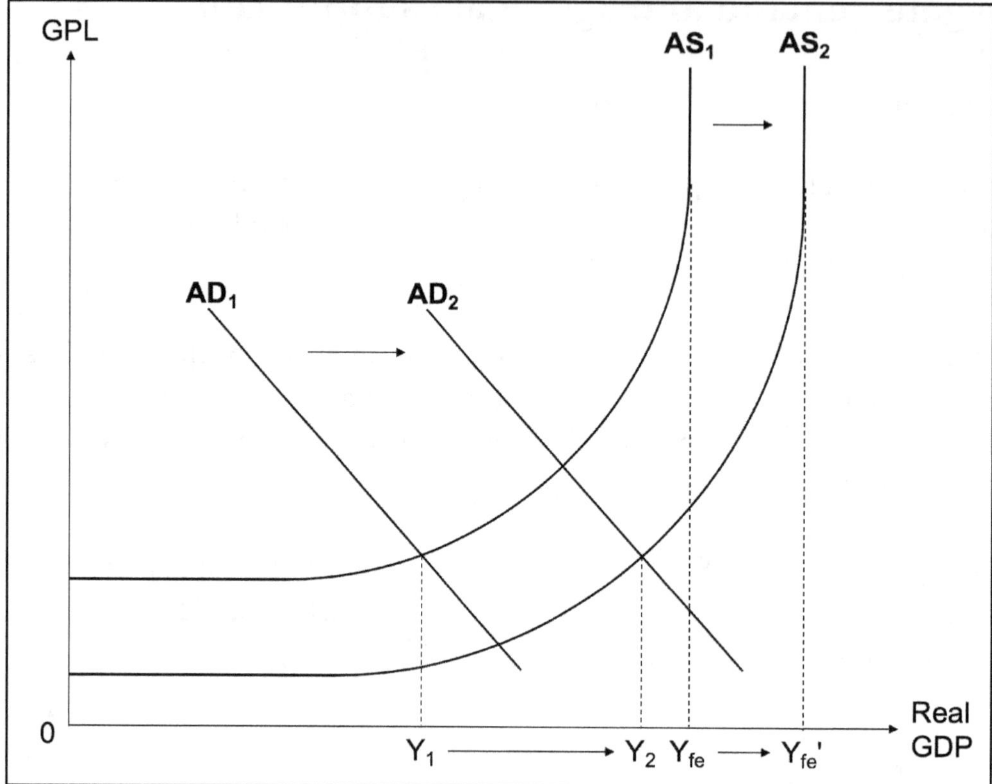

Fig. 6. An increase in Investment leading to increased AD and AS.

7. Explain the impact of automatic stabilisers in an economy. (10)

Introduction

1. Automatic stabilisers are counter-cyclical measures put in place to prevent excessive fluctuations in economic activity and to smooth out business cycles.

2. Such stabilisers constitute non-discretionary fiscal policy, in that they require no deliberate government action.

3. Two examples of automatic stabilisers are a progressive income tax structure and unemployment (UE) benefits.

Explanation of rise of AD & impacts on economy

1. For instance, the 2016 Summer Olympics in Rio de Janerio saw a massive influx of tourists, who contributed to soaring consumer and export expenditures. This would have likely led to a large increase in Aggregate Demand from AD_1 to AD_2 (as shown in Fig. 7 on the next page). With this increase, the excess AD at the original GPL creates a shortage of goods and services produced, causing an unplanned fall in inventories.

2. This in turn creates an upward pressure on prices, prompting profit-maximising firms to increase production, leading to a multiplied increase in Real Gross Domestic Product — via the multiplier process as an increase in incomes induces more spending which leads to further rounds of an increase in output and income.

3. Hence the economic output reaches a new equilibrium Y_2, and the price level increases to P_2 as well.

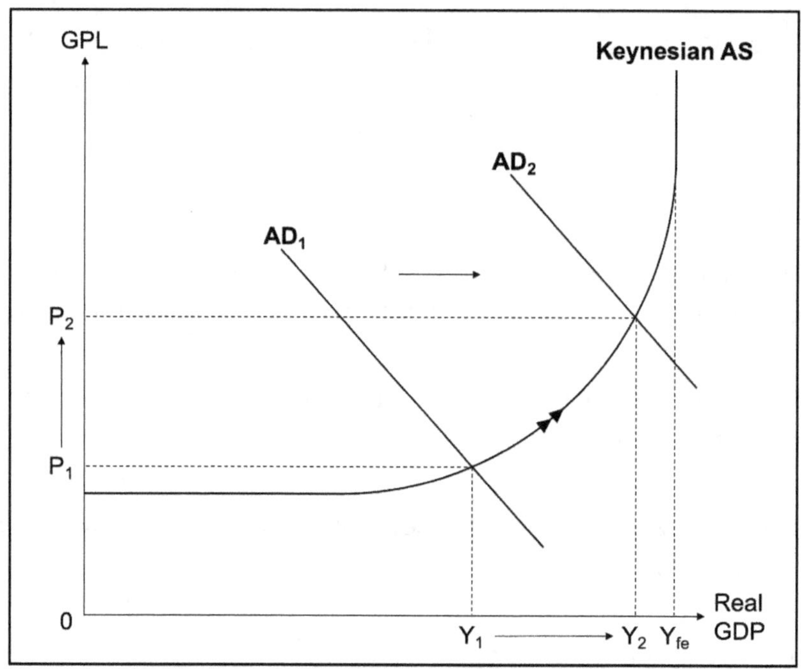

Fig. 7. The Effect of a Rise in AD on the Economy.

Stabiliser 1: Progressive income tax structure

1. Progressive income tax refers to a direct ad-valorem tax structure which requires income earners to pay out a higher marginal tax rate as their income level increases.

2. With a rise in AD, more households will enter into higher tax brackets due to their increased incomes. Therefore, these households would also have to pay higher percentages of their income in the form of taxes.

3. The rise in taxation slows down the rise in disposable income, thus causing the induced consumer expenditure to increase by a smaller extent, curtailing the extent of the overall increase in AD.

Stabiliser 2: Unemployment benefits

1. The increase in production level caused by the economic growth will correspond with increased derived demand for labour, which will see more people gaining employment.

2. As a result, there would be a fall in unemployment, leading to a fall in the amount of unemployment benefits being paid out. This leads to a smaller rise in disposable income, causing consumer expenditure to increase by a smaller extent.

Diagrammatic explanation of automatic stabilisers

1. The automatic stabilisers help to slow down the rate of economic growth, which reduces inflationary pressures (ensuring that the GPL does not increase that drastically) and therefore has a stabilising effect on the economy.

2. This can be seen from the diagram below where the rise in AD is dampened and AD_1 only increases to AD_3, rather than the original increase from AD_1 to AD_2.

3. Hence, GPL increases to a smaller extent (P_1 to P_3 instead of P_1 to P_2) and inflationary pressures are reduced.

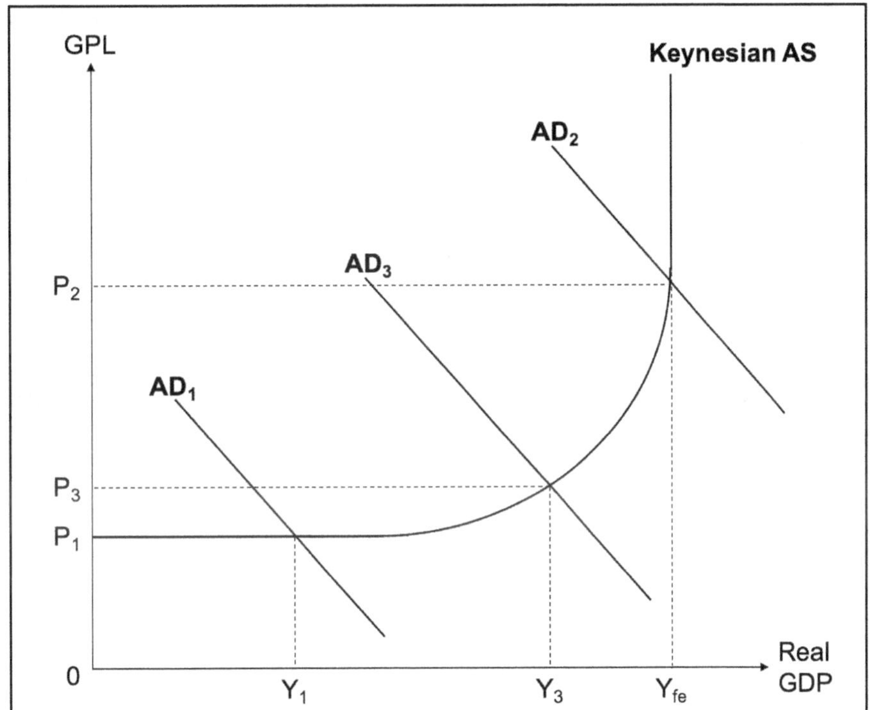

Fig. 8. Automatic Stabilisers dampening the magnitude of an Increase in AD.

Conclusion

1. If the economy experiences a contraction, the above-mentioned automatic stabilisers will achieve the opposite effect. As the income of households falls, they move into lower tax brackets and pay a lesser proportion of their income as taxes. Simultaneously, the fall in national output leads to a fall in derived DD for labour, leading to more people becoming unemployed and receiving UE benefits.

2. Taken together, the automatic stabilisers lead disposable income to fall by a smaller extent, causing consumer expenditure to decrease by a smaller extent.

8. Evaluate government policies that could be used to promote a more equal distribution of income. (15)

Introduction

1. The problem of inequality in income distribution arises because ownership of factors of production (FOPs) are highly unequal in the free market system, resulting in a vast inequality in factor incomes with some having unfair or no access to basic necessities.

2. Therefore, the pursuit of equity in the distribution of income is interpreted as the pursuit for greater equality relative to what would be achieved by the free market system.

3. This could be achieved through various government policies, including progressive taxation and redistribution, training and education, and price controls such as a minimum wage.

Policy 1: Progressive Taxation and redistribution

1. To promote greater equality in income distribution and thus equity, progressive taxation could be used as a tool to narrow income differences between the rich and the poor, and the resulting tax revenue could be redistributed to the poor through subsidies or transfer payments.

2. Progressive taxation refers to a system of direct taxation in which high income taxpayers pay a larger proportion of their income in taxes as compared to low income taxpayers. To further narrow income differences, such progressive taxation could also be extended to capital gains and interest incomes earned by the rich.

3. For example, the UK charges a 45% tax rate on incomes earned above £ 150,000 per year – taxing the rich more. However, the government allows for a deductible "personal allowance" amount of £ 11,850, for which no tax is charged. A low-income worker earning less than £ 11,850 a year would not need to pay income taxes at all.

4. Following which, the tax revenue could be redistributed to those most in need of money. For example, unemployment benefits could be given to those who are unable to find a job. Otherwise, subsidies on daily necessities could support low-income workers.

5. Transfer payments could also be given — for example in the case of Singapore, where the government dishes out consumption tax rebates to low-income households. Thus, the poor would effectively have reduced taxes on the goods and services which they purchase, allowing them to better afford daily necessities.

6. This policy is effective as it allows for the government to be targeted at helping the poor, through specialised programmes funded by increasing the taxes on high-income earners. The gap in disposable income narrows and thus serves to improve the equality in income distribution.

<u>Policy 1: Problems and Limitations</u>

1. However, one concern would be that such redistribution schemes could end up creating a 'crutch mentality' for low-income households. As the poor become more reliant on unemployment benefits and other support schemes, they may be disincentivised to work, and would rather simply collect handouts.

2. In the long-run, this creates significant problems for the government as it would have to devote more and more funds to support these low-income earners that are dependent on the government, placing a severe strain on the government's budget.

3. Additionally, this could hamper the productive growth of the economy, as a segment of the population becomes increasingly reliant on the government and thus are not incentivised to seek employment or upgrade their skills to seek better jobs.

4. Furthermore, the implementation of the progressive tax could also reduce the incentive to work, leading to a reduction in the effective labour supply. It could also lead to a brain drain. For example, the UK was infamous for implementing its "supertax" in the late 20th Century, which caused the effective tax rate on the highest-income earners to reach 95%. This created a massive disincentive to work as there is little additional disposable income to gain from additional work. This resulted in a massive "brain drain", as many Britons migrated to other countries with the hope of earning higher disposable incomes.

Policy 2: Training and Education Schemes

1. Training and Education policies are a form of supply-side policy aimed at boosting the skills of workers and ensuring that their skillsets remain relevant.

2. For example, the Singapore government has in place its SkillsFuture initiative, which provides a S$ 500 rebate for all Singaporeans to attend a variety of training courses.

3. Additionally, the Singapore government has also implemented the Workfare Training Support Scheme, that provides subsidies and allowances for attending courses to upgrade work skills. These are targeted at workers earning a gross monthly income below S$ 2000.

4. Such schemes target and particularly benefit low-income workers, providing them the opportunity to improve their skills and educate themselves in spite of their lack of money to do so, thus enabling them to work in higher-paying jobs in the future

5. Additionally, this policy also ensures that low-skilled, low-income workers are more protected from the threat of structural unemployment, and are better equipped to handle changes to the demand for skills.

Policy 2: Problems and Limitations

1. However, this policy has uncertain outcomes. Much is dependent on the workers themselves – their willingness to undergo training, their receptiveness to the training, their ability to upgrade, and even their awareness of the policy's existence.

2. Furthermore, the policy is likely to be subject to time lags as training takes some time. Also, changing the workers' mindsets will likely take a long time.

3. This policy is also subject to significant costs, in the form of the funds required to provide the subsidies, as well as to run the various programmes. This could place a strain on the government's budget, and hinder the government's ability to pursue other policies.

Policy 3: Minimum Wage

1. A minimum wage refers to a legally-imposed price floor in the labour market, ensuring that all workers receive at least a given wage per hour. For example, in the US, there is federal minimum wage at US$ 7.25 per hour.

2. This would be an effective wage floor in the market for low-skilled labour, where the equilibrium wage is below the minimum wage imposed. This hence serves to increase the wages of low-skilled, low-income workers, allowing them to better afford basic necessities such as housing, thereby improving equity.

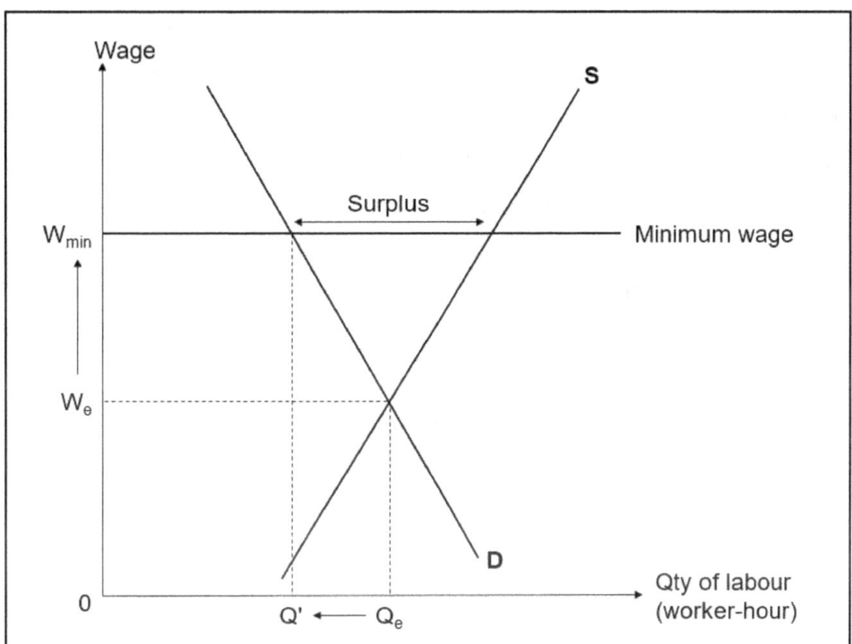

Fig. 9. Minimum Wage to promote Increased Equity.

3. Assuming that the demand for labour is relatively wage-inelastic, this causes the increase in wages accrued by low-income workers to be more-than-proportionate to the fall in quantity demanded for the workers. As a result, there is a net benefit to low-income workers, and the distribution of income is improved. Since this policy requires no expenditure on the government's part, it is also a relatively easier policy to implement and sustain than the previous two, with no fear of budgetary constraints.

Policy 3: Problems and Limitations

1. However, one concern with the minimum wage is that it would result in unemployment, as firms seek to cut costs and would thus retrench some workers, resulting in a decreased quantity of labour employed. As seen in Fig. 9 on the previous page, the minimum wage creates a permanent surplus of labour, as the quantity supplied of labour exceeds the quantity demanded of labour at W_{min}. The total amount of labour employed decreases from Qe to Q'. For the low-income workers retrenched as a result of this policy, they will be significantly worse off than before, with no income at all to support their daily needs.

2. There is also the fear that the minimum wage could incentivise firms to increase their automation to offset the increased labour costs, rendering more low-income jobs obsolete. For example, in recent years, the fast food chain McDonald's has been replacing cashiers and front-end service staff with new machines where customers can directly order their food.

3. Additionally, the minimum wage could result in a black market for labour, where low-income workers such as immigrants are forced to work unregulated jobs at wages below minimum wage. Such jobs operate outside the purview of the law, and thus could present safety or health risks to the workers concerned. Furthermore, the existence of such a black market would negate the minimum wage, thereby doing little to improve income distribution.

Concluding Section

1. In the pursuit of equity, the government could take multiple approaches. However, no one policy is the perfect solution.

2. Training and education schemes are, perhaps, the best long-term solution which allows low-income earners to break out of the poverty cycle.

3. This should be implemented hand-in-hand with a progressive tax system, and some form of redistribution through subsidies and transfer payments. However these should be well-calibrated to avoid the negative effects as explained.

4. On the other hand, a minimum wage policy is much more controversial, with its merits and demerits being less clear in the real world. A Singapore version, the Progressive Wage Model, which sets sector-specific minimum wage for a few specific sectors as well as wage ladders tied in with training, could be a more targeted though complex alternative to consider.

9. Discuss the possible consequences of unemployment (15)

Introduction

1. Unemployment of labour occurs when people who are willing and able to work, are actively seeking but unable to find employment.

Wastage of Scarce Resources

1. Unemployment constitutes a waste of the scarce resource of labour. With workers being unable to work, the economy would be producing below full-employment output level.

2. With reference to Fig. 10 below, an economy without unemployment would be producing at a point along the PPC, such as Point A — fully utilising all available resources (labour, especially) to produce the maximum number of capital and consumer goods in any particular combination.

3. However, given unemployment within an economy, it would be producing at a point inside the Production Possibility Curve, such as point B — underutilising the available labour resources, and thereby producing at output levels below the maximum amount it could produce.

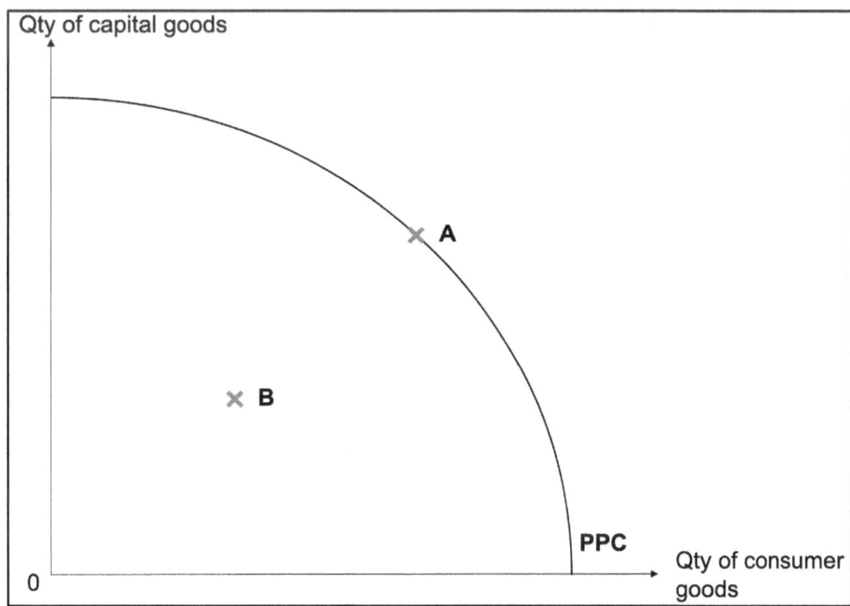

Fig. 10. A Production Possibilities Curve illustrating Under-Production.

4. As a result, fewer goods are produced in the economy, satisfying fewer wants, and leading to a lower standard of living.

Fall in Economic Growth

1. Unemployment means people do not earn income and therefore would be unwilling to spend as much as before on goods and services. As their savings deplete, this will lead to greater fall in consumer expenditure, which is a component of the Aggregate Demand (AD).

2. At the same time, firms would also cut back on their investment as a result of lowered confidence in economy leading to reduced expected rates of returns on investment projects. Thus, the Investment component of AD could also be falling.

3. Diagrammatically, this is represented by the decrease in Aggregate Demand from AD_1 to AD_2 in Fig. 11 on the next page.

4. Concurrently, a high rate of long-term unemployment would reduce both the quantity and quality of the labour force.

5. The longer people remain unemployed, the greater the chances of them losing their skills. The loss of proficiency in skills occurs because the unemployed are not actively using them. Hence, this results in lower productivity and a fall in the quality of the labour force.

6. Furthermore, unemployed workers might become discouraged after a long-period without being able to obtain a job. Should such discouraged workers cease the job search altogether, they effectively drop-out of the labour force and become "not economically active", leading to a fall in the quantity of labour available.

7. The fall in the quantity and quality of the labour force, a Factor of Production, would shrink the productive capacity, reducing the full-employment output level of the economy. As seen in Fig. 11 on the next page, the Long-Run part of the Keynesian AS curve would shift leftwards from AS to AS', decreasing the full employment level of output from Y_f to Y_f'.

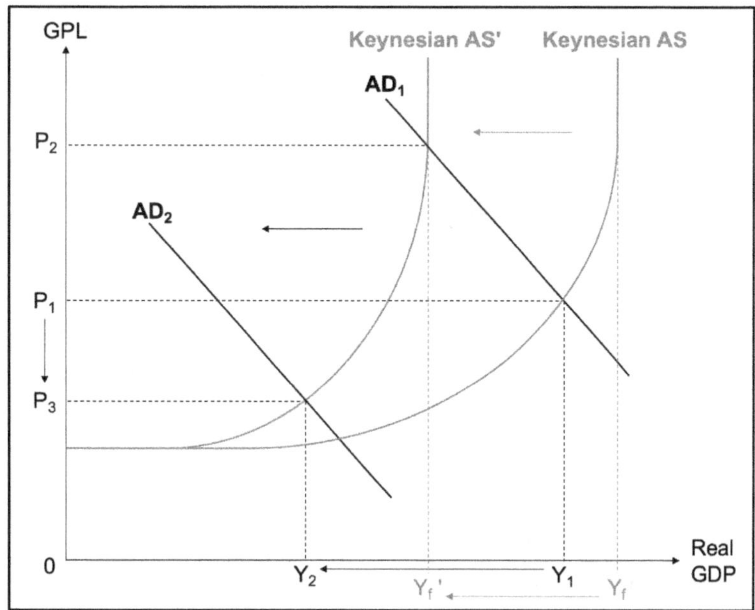

Fig. 11. Long-Term Unemployment leading to a decrease in AD and AS.

8. The combined effect of a fall in AD and a fall in AS would lead to a drastic fall in the actual output of the economy, from Y_1 to Y_2, and a fall in the potential output as well, from Y_f to Y_f'.

<u>Decline in the Government's Budget</u>

1. The unemployed do not earn an income and therefore would pay little to no income taxes. This results in a loss of tax revenue for the government. At the same time, the government would also have to incur a higher expenditure because of the increased amount of unemployment welfare benefits they have to give out.

2. Thus, with tax revenue reduced and government expenditure increasing, this places a strain on the government's budget.

3. Therefore, the government would have less funds available for alternative uses such as the provision of public goods like anti-flood systems and merit goods like hospital care. This can lead to flooding, reduced quality or access to healthcare, as well as other inconveniences to living. Along with the fact that unemployment may also cause social problems such as rising crime rates, this means that there would be a fall in the non-material standard of living, which concerns the less-tangible quality of life factors.

4. Additionally, this decline in the government's budget is even more concerning because it hampers the government's ability to enact policies that deal with the unemployment, possibly allowing for a vicious cycle to take hold.

Reduced susceptibility to overheating

1. However, unemployment may also lead to some positive consequences. By definition, unemployment entails that there will be some spare capacity in the economy. Hence, should AD increase in the future, it is not going to cause the economy to overheat, since firms can employ the idle resources in order to expand production.

2. If there was zero unemployment in the first place, any increase in AD would lead to intense competition for labour, causing wages to increase intensely and leading to demand-pull inflation and subsequent wage-price spirals. This can be unhealthy as money would be rapidly losing value and the situation can spiral into an economic crisis.

Spur Entrepreneurship

1. By virtue of necessity, the unemployed may be forced to find means and ways to earn an income. This can lead to some starting a business and eventually becoming a successful entrepreneur that in turn contributes to jobs for others. As entrepreneurship is a factor of production, the spurring of entrepreneurship can thus result in greater economic growth in the long-term.

Aid in Economic Restructuring

1. From time to time, there may be some need to restructure the economy away from certain sectors to other new sectors. For example, the Government may see it fit to diversify the economy from being agricuture-dependent and hence decide to build up a manufacturing base. Such economic plans could be hampered if all workers are already employed. Now, the unemployed can be possibly sent for training, sponsored by the Government and with some training allowance earned. In this way, the skills of the workforce will be increasing, making it possible to attract foreign direct investments (since relevant skills are available), and build up a manufacturing base, aiding in the economic restructuring efforts.

Concluding Section

1. Overall, unemployment leads to far more severe negative consequences than there are positive ones.

2. That is why Governments in general have the macroeconomic goal of full employment.

3. The positive impacts of unemployment (achievement of economic restructuring, increased entrepreneurship and reduced susceptibility to overheating) can be brought about through deliberate government policies, without having to experience the consequences associated with greater unemployment.

10. Discuss the role of investment in promoting economic growth. (15)

Introduction

1. Economic growth refers to the increase in the value of goods and services produced by an economy and consists of actual and potential economic growth. Actual growth is the annual percentage increase in the real GDP or output of an economy. Potential growth refers to the rate at which the economy could grow at if all resources were efficiently employed.

2. Investment refers to expenditure by firms on new capital goods such as factories and machinery.

Thesis 1: Investments play a major role in helping achieve sustained and non-inflationary EG

1. Increased investment leads to actual and potential economic growth.

2. For example, the smartphone maker Apple, an American company, has been conducting FDI into China's economy, setting up regional production centres in China by acquiring capital goods such as factories and machinery. This would increase investment expenditure (I) in China's economy, ceteris paribus. Consequently, this would lead to an increase in the level of Aggregate Demand (AD) in the economy.

3. The increased AD creates a shortage of goods and services at the original general price level, placing an upward pressure on prices, incentivising firms to increase the actual output, constituting actual economic growth.

4. This initial increase in real output induces further increases in Aggregate Demand, through a process known as the Keynesian multiplier effect. As real output increases due to the initial FDI inflow, consumers enjoy greater disposable income, and firms enjoy increased profits — thereby allowing consumers to further increase C and firms to further increase I. Hence, increases in AD are compounded.

5. Simultaneously, this investment into China's economy serves to increase the capital stock of the economy. An increased number of factories and machinery, as well as improvements to existing factories, serve to increase the quantity and quality of Factors of Production (FOPs), and allowing existing factors to become more productive. For example, the new machineries could utilise more advanced technology, requiring fewer units of factor inputs (such as worker-hours, electricity, raw materials etc) to produce the same amount of output.

6. Thus, the productive capacity of the economy expands, causing the long-run and the short-run parts of the AS to increase, with a corresponding rise in the full-employment level of output, hence constituting potential economic growth.

7. This is as reflected in Fig. 12 below. AD increases from AD_1 to AD_2, driven by the influx of FDI into the economy. This in turn causes an increase in the Keynesian AS, due to the increase in capital stock of the economy. As a result, the economy experiences both actual growth (from Y_1 to Y_2) and potential growth (from Y_{fe} to Y_{fe}') — with no corresponding increase in the General Price Level, which remains constant at P_1.

8. Hence investment can bring about both actual growth and potential growth and help achieve sustained & non-inflationary economic growth.

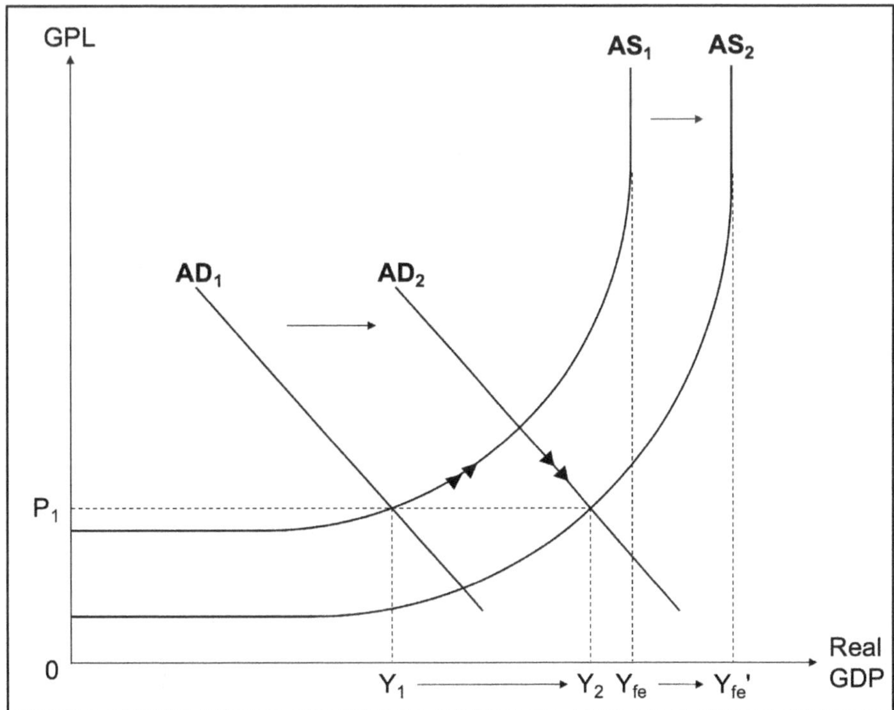

Fig. 12. Investments leading to increased AD and AS.

Thesis 2: A Fall in Investments may reduce Productive Capacity and lead to negative EG rates

1. To illuminate the critical role that investments play in productive growth, let us consider what would happen should investment expenditures decrease.

2. A fall in investment levels causes a corresponding decrease in Capital accumulation within the economy. This will reduce potential growth rates, which translates to poorer long-term growth prospects.

3. With stunted potential growth, there is a high risk that actual growth rates would outpace potential growth rates, leading to a situation where resources in the economy become increasingly scarce and eventually the actual economic output becomes constrained by the lagging potential growth.

4. Investment expenditures need not even decrease to bring about such a situation. As long as investment levels are insufficient to replace worn-out or obsolete Capital goods, then this effectively causes the amount of Capital goods in economy to shrink. Thusly, productive capacity shrinks, translating to decreases in AS which would create deflationary pressures within the economy, potentially leading to negative actual growth rates.

5. Thus it is evident that investments are crucial in ensuring sustained actual and potential growth within the economy.

Thesis 3: FDI is especially critical for ELDCs

1. Foreign direct investment (FDI) refers to investment by firms based in one country (the home country) in productive activities in another country (the host country).

2. Economically Less-Developed Countries (ELDCs) are characterised by high poverty rates, low GDP, and poor infrastructure. FDI is able to address these above-mentioned issues by plugging the investment gap that fundamentally exists within ELDCs.

3. When a firm conducts FDI into an ELDC, this is often accompanied by the transfer of technical and managerial expertise, as well as new production technologies, which can be learned and adopted by the local labour force (workers and managers) and local businesses. This involves technological improvements as well as improvements in human capital (the acquisition of new skills and knowledge by the local labour force), which improve the productivity and quality of existing FOPs, leading to increased potential output.

4. Should the firms conducting FDI need to pay taxes to the host country's government, this would also give the governments of ELDCs increased budgetary freedom to enact policies that boost economic growth.

5. An influx of FDI into an ELDC from various developed countries also creates the possibility of opening trade relationships with these developed countries, which are able to provide a ready export market for the ELDC to take advantage of. With export expenditures increasing, this would cause AD and thus real output to rise as well, constituting actual growth.

6. Hence, investments are very critical in helping ELDCs achieve growth.

<u>Anti-Thesis 1: Investment is a small & volatile component</u>

1. However, investment is often volatile and dependent on business sentiment, which can fluctuate wildly.

2. For example, the UK's recent decision to leave the European Union has caused a massive drop in investment levels in its economy, to the tune of £ 22 billion over the two and a half years since the decision was made. This is despite the fact that Brexit has not yet even been finalised.

3. This goes to show that investment expenditures are largely subject to business sentiment, which can change at any moment and can have no correlation to economic performance or the underlying strength of an economy in general.

4. Moreover, investment expenditure as a % of GDP generally stands at around 20%. Hence, it may not be a significant and consistent driver of EG.

5. For large and open economies, consumption expenditure is usually the most significant component of AD, making up 68.14% of the US economy's real GDP in 2018. For small and open economies, net export revenue is another significant factor to take into account, with the Singapore economy seeing 26.56% of its real GDP coming from net exports in 2018. These components of AD could therefore be more important drivers of economic growth.

Anti-Thesis 2: Investments cannot be relied upon for economic recovery

1. Where economic recovery is necessary, for instance in the aftermath of an economic crash or a recession (where economic growth rates are negative), investments cannot be relied upon to stimulate growth.

2. With a trend of negative growth rates, investors and business would (understandably) have a pessimistic business outlook, wary of the possibility of even further declines in real GDP.

3. In such cases, the onus is on the government to directly stimulate the economy through Government expenditure (G), a component of AD, in addition to implementing other policies that aid in economic recovery.

Anti-Thesis 3: Investments cannot be solely relied upon for potential growth

1. In order to ensure consistent potential growth, deliberate government policies are needed to increase the quantity and quality of FOPs — Land, Labour, Capital, Entrepreneurship.

2. However, investments are only able to directly target the improvement of Capital goods, which are but one of several FOPs.

3. Governmental policies, on the other hand, are able to increase the quantity and quality of Land, Labour, Capital and Entrepreneurship.

4. Pro-immigration policies would allow the expansion of the labour base, while incentive schemes and direct provision of training and education would increase the quality of Labour. Research and Development (R&D) grants and other small business subsidies would go a long way towards enticing entrepreneurs to establish their own businesses, improving both the quantity and quality of Entrepreneurship. And proper legislation mandating sustainable farming practices would ensure the sustainability and thus the continued quality of Land resources. All these policies would improve potential growth.

5. Additionally, firms also cannot be entirely relied upon to provide all necessary capital goods. For instance, the construction of large-scale infrastructure (such as railways, expressways, telecommunications networks) is often carried out by the government, which has to step in due to huge national scale of such projects, and the positive externalities involved. Such infrastructure would enable large increases in productivity, and are thus critical to enabling both potential and actual growth.

6. Thus, it is evident that in the way of potential growth, it is government policies that are the most important factor.

<u>Anti-Thesis 4: Over-Investment carries severe consequences</u>

1. Furthermore, there is also the risk that over-investment may occur, as it did in the Chinese economy around the period 2009-2012.

2. In the case of the Chinese, state-owned enterprises flushed with funds and cheap credit pursued relentless expansion plans, fuelling a construction boom and sparking off high levels of economic growth initially.

3. But this economic growth was fundamentally unsustainable. Investment expenditures were spent acquiring/building capital goods for which there was little demand or purpose. These so-called "Mis-Investments" caused factories and capital goods to be left idle — a wastage of scarce resources.

4. In turn, such investment projects drew little in the way of returns. The investment firms became saddled with debts and many turned bankrupt and shut down. In turn, this caused many rounds of worker layoffs and/or wage cuts, in turn leading to a fall in purchasing power of the average consumer, reducing C and hence stunting economic growth.

5. It is also possible that too high a level of investments may lead to economic growth that is unsustainable. For example, high levels of investment into the mining industry might lead to the construction of too many mine factories, which will lead to a rapid depletion of mineral resources.

6. In such cases, these investments may have provided a lucrative and effective source of economic growth in the short term, but there is the risk that governments would grow overly-reliant on such unsustainable sources to drive high growth rates.

7. When these natural resources inevitably run out, the economy may not be yet equipped to pursue growth through other means (e.g. manufacturing), hence posing a great danger that the short-term economic boom enjoyed at present may come at the expense of a long-term, sustainable and healthy economic growth.

Concluding Section

1. Investment plays a critical role in achieving sustained and non-inflationary economic growth, as it has the unique capacity to bring about increases in both AD and AS simultaneously.

2. But at the same time, other components of the AD are equally important as they tend to be more significant engines for growth.

3. Perhaps government policies are most the most important factor overall. Appropriate policies are needed to create and ensure a conducive economic environment for attracting investments, as well as to keep the other engines of economic growth firing, and to continually increase the quantity and quality of FOPs to ensure continued potential (and hence, actual) growth.

11. Explain what enables rapid economic growth. (10)

Introduction

1. Economic growth is a macroeconomic goal of all countries, and is defined as the increase in the value of all the final goods and services produced in an economy, over time.

2. Overall, a rapid economic growth can only be achieved with a combination of a few factors — a large initial rise in Aggregate Demand, a large Multiplier value and the presence of sufficient spare capacity in the economy.

Large Initial Autonomous Rise in AD needed

1. Firstly, a large increase in AD would be necessary to have rapid economic growth.

2. There is a positive relationship between the extent of increase in AD and actual economic growth. As illustrated in Fig. 13, when AD only experiences a marginal boost from AD_1 to AD_2, the real GDP of the economy correspondingly sees only a small increase from Y_1 to Y_2. In contrast, a large boost in AD from AD_1 to AD_3 would drive a more rapid and pronounced spike in real GDP from Y_1 to Y_3.

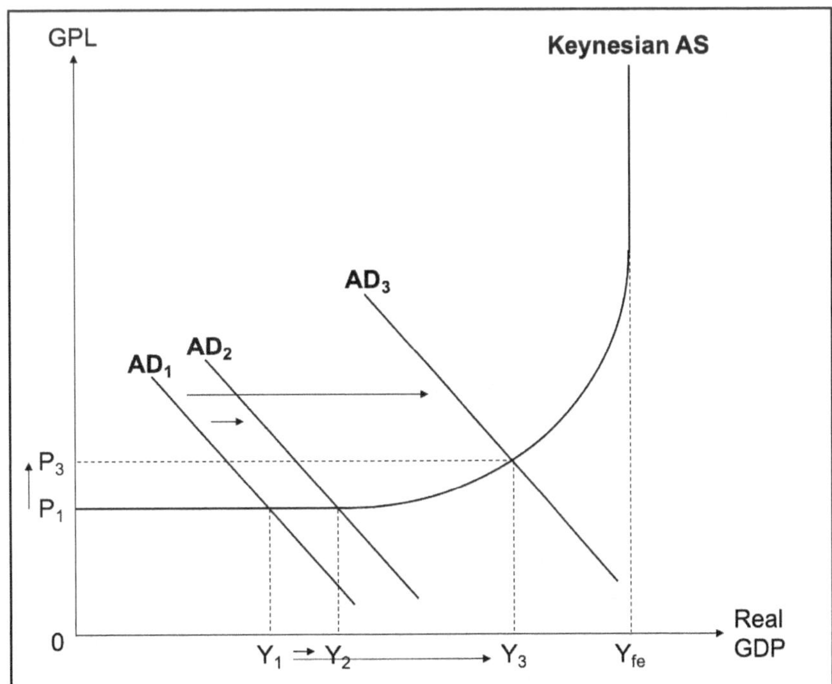

Fig. 13. Comparing Extent of Increase in AD on economic growth.

3. Such a scenario involving a large increase in AD is likely to occur if several or all components of the AD, C, I, G and (X – M), is increasing.

4. A rise in confidence in the economy would make households more willing to spend on goods and services, hence increasing consumption.

5. Firms with greater business confidence would also see higher expected rates of return on investment projects and hence they would invest more due to the projected profits of the investment.

6. An increase in government spending on infrastructure or other public works could also increase the G component, increasing AD.

7. Furthermore, the net exports component can increase if there is overseas economic growth that led foreign purchasing power to increase, hence allowing foreigners to increase their demand for the country's exports, increasing export revenue and the net export revenue component of AD.

Large multiplier value

1. With a large multiplier (k > 1), given the same increase in AD or Aggregate Expenditure (AE), the increase in real GDP (rGDP) and hence economic growth rate would be greater. This can be seen through the formula —

$$\Delta rGDP = k\Delta AE$$

2. This is because a large multiplier value occurs when marginal propensity of withdrawal (MPW) is low. This can be seen through the formula —

$$k = \frac{1}{MPW}$$

3. A low MPW could arise, for instance, due to a consumerist culture, which would cause the Marginal Propensity to Save to be very low as households prefer to spend rather than save any potential increases in income.

4. With a low MPW, more of the increase in income is funnelled back into the circular flow by means of induced consumption, rather than being leaked out of the economy as savings, taxes or imports]. This in turn will lead a greater increase in output and more rounds of income generation and more spending.

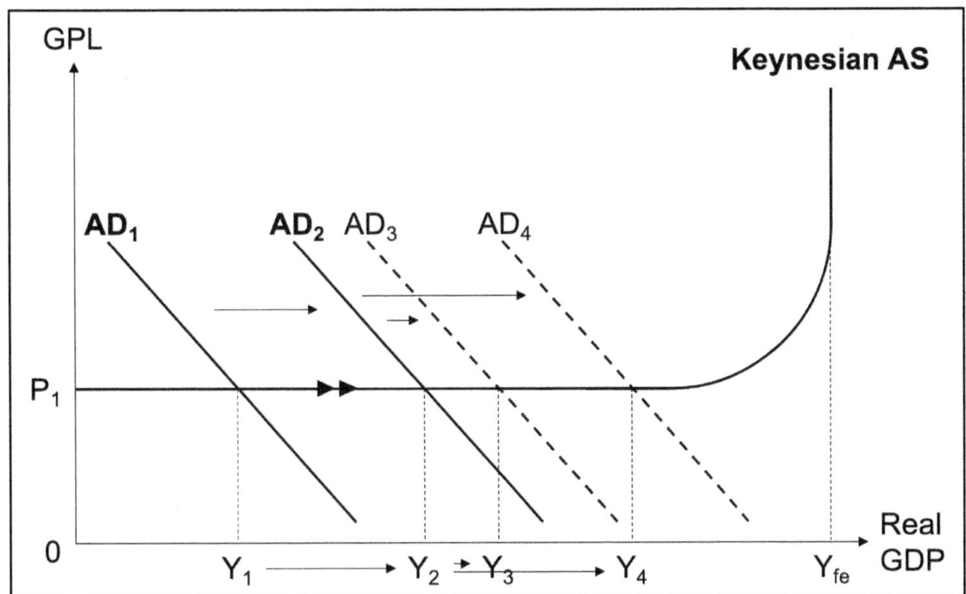

Fig. 14. Illustrating the difference between a Small and a Large Keynesian Multiplier.

5. As is illustrated in Fig. 14, given the same initial increase in autonomous spending from AD_1 to AD_2, this initial increase would go on to induce more spending through the multiplier effect.

6. Should the Keynesian multiplier value be of a low magnitude, this subsequent induced spending would represent only a small increase in AD from AD_2 to AD_3. Conversely, with a high Keynesian multiplier value, the induced spending causes a large increase in AD from AD_2 to AD_4.

7. As can be seen, the overall growth rate with a low multiplier value (Y_1 to Y_3) is significantly smaller than it would be with a higher multiplier value (Y_1 to Y_4). Hence, it is evident that a higher multiplier value enables a faster growth rate.

Adequate Spare Capacity

1. Finally, even with a large increase in AD and a large multiplier size, rapid economic growth may not occur if there is a lack of spare capacity to accommodate the increasing AD.

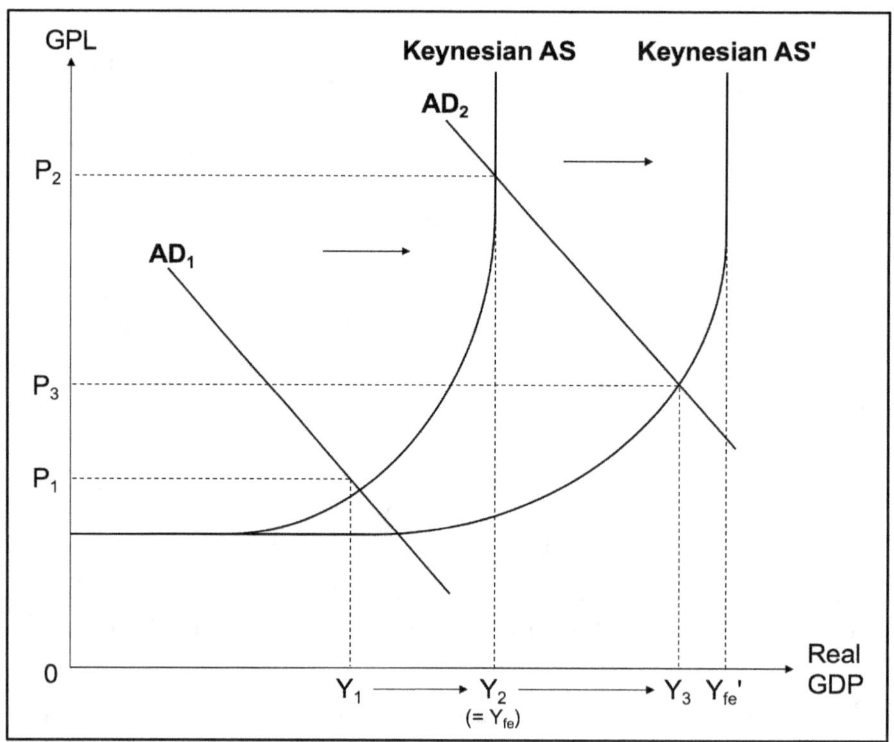

Fig. 15. Comparing the extent of Actual Growth with and without Potential Growth.

2. For instance, consider the case where a significant increase in AD occurs with no corresponding change to the productive capacity of the economy. As seen in Fig. 15, with AD rising exponentially from AD_1 to AD_2, real output would increase from Y_1 to Y_2 and the economy would have reached its full-employment output level on the Keynesian AS curve. At this point, no spare capacity exists within the economy, and further increases in AD can no longer trigger economic growth, and would merely serve to bid up prices.

3. However, when potential growth occurs alongside actual growth, not only is the actual growth rate increased, but it also allows for spare capacity to exist and for future increases in real output. With AD and AS increasing in tandem, actual growth would be greater (from Y_1 to Y_3), and the economy would still have the capacity for future growth (represented by the gap between Y_3 and Y_{fe}'). Therefore, to enable rapid economic growth, there should also be increases in the long run part of aggregate supply; in other words, potential economic growth.

4. This can be brought about by increasing the quality and quantity of factors of production. For example, if there is immigration of foreign labour, the quantity of labour factors (i.e. the size of the labour force) would increase. Furthermore, if these immigrants constitute "foreign talents" or skilled labour, the quality of labour factors would also increase, increasing the productive capacity.

5. Alternatively, large-scale infrastructure projects (often financed by the government) is able to spur both actual and potential growth. For instance, the construction of a national highway system. The significantly increased government expenditures to finance this highway construction project would in and of itself bring about increases in AD (as G is a component of AS). Meanwhile, the highways being built would facilitate reduced transportation costs and the productive man-hours lost to traffic congestion on a daily basis. This improves the quantity and quality of existing Factors of Production, allowing for increased productive capacity and hence actual growth..

12. Compare and contrast the effectiveness of Fiscal policy and Monetary policy in dealing with a recession. (15)

Introduction

1. A recession is defined as two consecutive quarters of negative economic growth.

Fiscal Policy

1. Fiscal policy refers to the deliberate use of government spending and taxation to influence aggregate demand.

2. Expansionary fiscal policy, in particular, involves increasing government spending (G) and reducing taxes.

3. As G is a component of the AD (AD = C + I + G + (X – M)), an increase in G will lead to a corresponding increase in AD.

4. A fall in personal income tax rates will lead to higher disposable incomes available to households. With greater disposable income and hence increased purchasing power, consumption increases.

5. A fall in corporate income tax rate will lead to an increase in after-tax profits, which raises the expected rate of return on investment projects, as well as provide the firms with more funds (from the profits) for investment. Firms are hence more likely to invest, resulting in a rise in investment expenditure I.

6. As both C and I increases, AD increases. The rise in AD will hence help to combat the deflationary pressures experienced by the economy during the recession.

Monetary Policy (based on interest rates)

1. On the other hand, monetary policy refers to deliberate action taken by a country's central bank to alter the country's money supply, interest rate or exchange rate to influence AD.

2. Expansionary monetary policy, in particular, involves increasing the money supply in order to cut interest rates.

3. With interest rates decreasing, the rate of returns on savings would also decreases, thereby reducing the opportunity cost of consumption and hence encouraging increased consumption.

4. At the same time, the cost of borrowing falls, which incentivises consumers to borrow and spend more. With a decreased cost of borrowing, the expected rate of returns to investment projects would increase, thereby increasing the number of profitable investment projects available to firms. This incentivises investment activities by firms, hence leading to an increase in I.

5. The increases in C and I consequently lead to a corresponding increase in AD.

<u>Secondary Effect of Monetary Policy on Exchange Rates</u>

1. In addition, the fall in interest rates leads to a fall in the expected rate of returns of depositing funds in the country's banks.

2. This results in a fall in hot money inflows and a rise in hot money outflows.

3. This, in turn, translates to a fall in the demand for and a rise in the supply of the country's currency. Therefore, this leads to a depreciation of the currency, ceteris paribus.

4. Hence, the price of exports in terms of foreign currency falls and the price of imports in terms of domestic currency rises. More exports are produced and sold as the exports become more price-competitive.

5. At the same time, domestic consumption increases as households switch away from relatively more expensive imports to the relatively cheaper domestically produced goods.

6. This leads to a rise in net exports (X – M) and a corresponding increase in AD, which helps to tackle the recession.

Similarities

1. Fiscal and monetary policies share multiple similarities in their effectiveness in dealing with a recession.

2. For one, both policies rely on the C and I components to increase AD and hence they are dependent on the confidence levels of consumers and firms. During a recession, households may simply prioritise saving over spending, in anticipation of emergencies like job losses. Similarly, firms may choose not to invest in spite of the policies as the prospects of the investment projects are generally dim due to the recession, thereby making it a highly risky financial endeavour for the firms to undertake in a time of uncertainty.

3. The effectiveness of both policies are also dependent on the magnitude of the multiplier effect evident within the specific economy in question. If the multiplier effect is larger, a given increase in AD would induce greater subsequent induced increases in spending, leading to an overall larger rise in real GDP, increasing the effectiveness of the policy.

4. The effectiveness of both policies are also affected by the extent of spare capacity. Although AD levels typically fall during a recession, this does not imply the existence of spare capacity within the economy. The productive capacity of the economy is likely to also decrease during the recession. (This could be due to various factors, such as the destruction of physical capita;, or the de-skilling of unemployed workers.) Consequently, the economy might still be operating at or near full capacity. This therefore limits the extent to which economic growth can be brought about through increases in AD alone — thereby effectively limiting the effectiveness of Fiscal and Monetary Policies as tools to combat the recession.

Differences

1. The effectiveness of Fiscal policy may be dependent on the state of the government's budget, whereby a government in a poor budgetary position would usually be unable to increase G and reduce taxes by a significant extent, and thus the policy will be less effective. On the other hand, Monetary Policy does not require government funds, thereby allowing it to be implemented regardless of the government's present budgetary position.

2. Fiscal policy is also affected by the crowding-out effect. By increasing G and reducing taxes, the government may have a budget deficit. Hence, there may be a need to borrow money by selling bonds to the public. The supply of loanable funds decreases leading to an increase in interest rate. This in turn leads to a fall in C and I, which may offset the rise in G, hence making the policy ineffective. Once again, Monetary Policy avoids such outcomes by simply not requiring the use of government funds.

3. There may be greater certainty in the effectiveness of the Fiscal policy as it includes the increased spending of the Government. Hence, even if household and firms do not increase their spending, there is still the certainty of AD increasing through the G component. On the other hand, the effectiveness of Monetary Policy is not as concrete, due to the fact that there is no direct injection of funds into the economy.

4. Fiscal policy tends to suffer from longer time lags than monetary policy. This is because there is a need for the Government to agree on what to increase spending on and where to impose tax cuts. This process can take a rather long time especially if there are political conflicts hampering the process. On the other hand, most central banks are non-partisan and operate independent of the legislative branches of government and its policy-making machinery. Therefore, central banks can typically make swift and unilateral decisions on Monetary policy. Especially in times of a recession, such time lags can make the difference between combating an economic downturn at its onset, and playing a fruitless game of catch-up in an already-dire economy.

5. While Fiscal policy does not boost net exports, Monetary policy in an open economy may result in such a boost (as explained above in the "Secondary Effects" section). Thus, if the economy is more reliant on exports for economic growth, in particular small and open economies, Monetary policy can provide a much greater impact on economic growth and thus prove to be critical in tackling the recession.

6. Unlike Fiscal policy, Monetary policy is affected by the liquidity trap, whereby an increase in money supply will no longer bring about a fall in interest rate. This usually occurs when the country's present interest rate is near zero, and thus the interest rate is unable to fall further by any significant extent. As a result, this places a 'limit' on the extent to which Monetary Policy can truly spur economic growth.

Concluding Section

1. Fiscal and monetary policies have different strengths and weaknesses.

2. To ensure greater effectiveness, we can combine both policies so that they can complement each other.

3. For example, the fiscal policy may result in crowding out effect which leads to a rise in interest rate, but that can be countered by implementing the monetary policy at the same time.

4. In addition, as fiscal policy includes the certainty of an increase in Government spending, this can boost the prevailing economic prospects, which in turn causes households and firms to be more responsive to the monetary policy.

13. Account for the increasing income gap between skilled and unskilled labour in Singapore. (10)

Introduction

1. The increasing income gap between skilled and unskilled labour is fundamentally caused by a widening wage gap between skilled and unskilled workers.

2. Such wages are determined by free market forces of demand and supply of labour, assuming the labour market is perfectly competitive.

Wage Inequality: a Demand and Supply Analysis

1. There are several factors that determine the demand for labour, including skill-level and demand for the final good.

2. As high-skilled workers will tend to be more productive, there is a greater demand for such workers compared to low-skilled workers.

3. To become a high-skilled worker, much aptitude is required as well as the willingness to undergo long periods of education and training, which also means that higher opportunity costs are incurred due to work and income foregone. As a result, there are fewer workers willing and able to put in the time and effort to undergo such training, therefore the supply of high-skilled workers will tend to be lower than the supply of low-skilled workers.

4. This is as illustrated in Fig. 16 on the next page. Given the higher demand and lower supply of high-skilled workers, the equilibrium wage for high-skilled labour will far exceed that of low-skilled labour, resulting in a large wage gap.

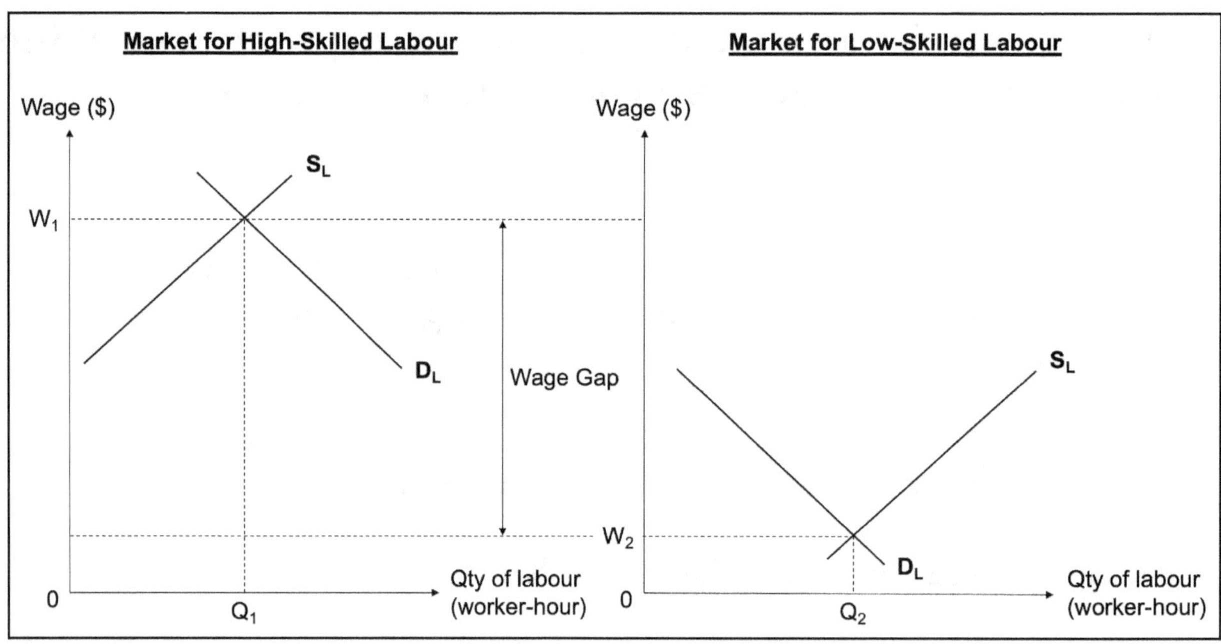

Fig. 16. Comparing the High-Skilled (left) and Low-Skilled (right) Labour Markets.

<u>Globalisation and technological advancement increases demand for skilled labour, widening the income gap</u>

1. Globalisation has increased the markets for Singapore's exports as more countries reduce their trade barriers and open up to freer trade.

2. As Singapore's comparative advantage lies in knowledge-intensive industries, exports of pharmaceutical, bio-medical and financial goods and services are among the sectors that have grown most rapidly alongside with globalisation.

3. As these sectors grow, so does the demand for skilled labour such as laboratory research personnel and wealth managers.

4. Technological advancement has also increased the demand for skilled labour.

5. This is because skilled labour is required to operate machinery, computers and other mechanised equipment brought about by technological advancement. Skilled labour is also needed to enable the utilisation of cutting-edge technologies such as artificial intelligence, cloud computing etc.

6. Thus the demand for skilled labour has increased tremendously, resulting in a significant increase in equilibrium wages of skilled labour, ceteris paribus.

7. The wage elasticity of supply of skilled labour is relatively inelastic as it takes a long time to educate and train up skilled labour.

8. As such, for the given increase in demand for skilled labour, wages of skilled labour is likely to increase more-than-proportionately to the increase in the quantity of workers employed as seen in Fig. 17 below.

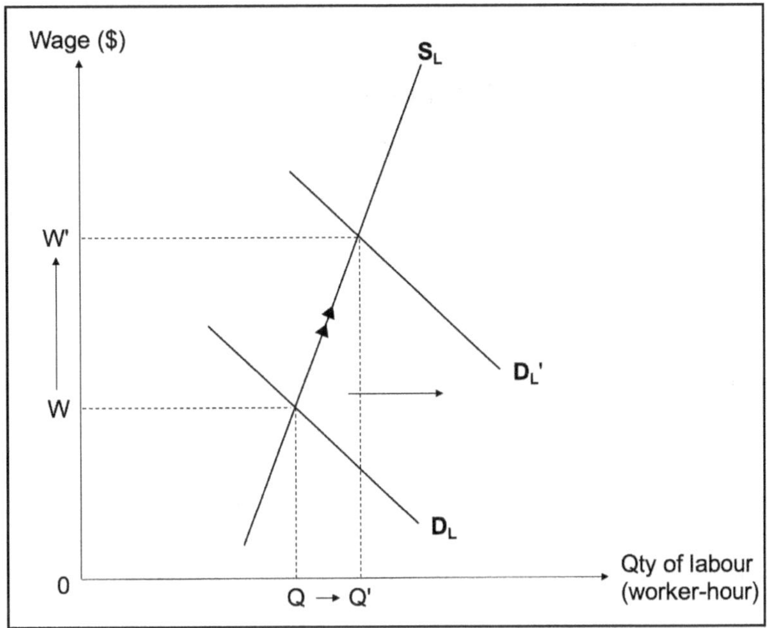

Fig. 17. The Market for Skilled Labour.

9. This further contributes to the huge increase in wages for skilled workers which exacerbates the income gap between skilled and unskilled labour.

10. In addition, due to global competition for talent and the freer movement of labour brought about by globalisation, the supply for skilled labour would not increase by much, as some locals migrate to take up job opportunities elsewhere in the world.

<u>Globalisation and technological advancement causes wages of unskilled labour to fall</u>

1. Globalisation has increased the supply of unskilled labour in Singapore. Freer movement of labour is a characteristic of globalisation. Singapore augments its supply of unskilled labour by allowing foreign workers to work in Singapore. Unskilled labour is deployed in various labour intensive industries such as cleaning services industry.

2. At the same time, technological advancements have decreased the demand for unskilled labour. Innovative inventions such as labour-saving machinery in cleaning industries that can run on artificial intelligence have substituted unskilled labour in certain applications for example.

3. With a decrease in the demand for unskilled labour and an increase in the supply of unskilled labour, a fall in the wages of unskilled labour will occur.

4. This can be seen in Fig. 18, with the demand for unskilled labour decreasing from D_L to D_L' and supply increasing from S_L to S_L'. This, in turn, creates a surplus at initial wage W, driving down wages to W'.

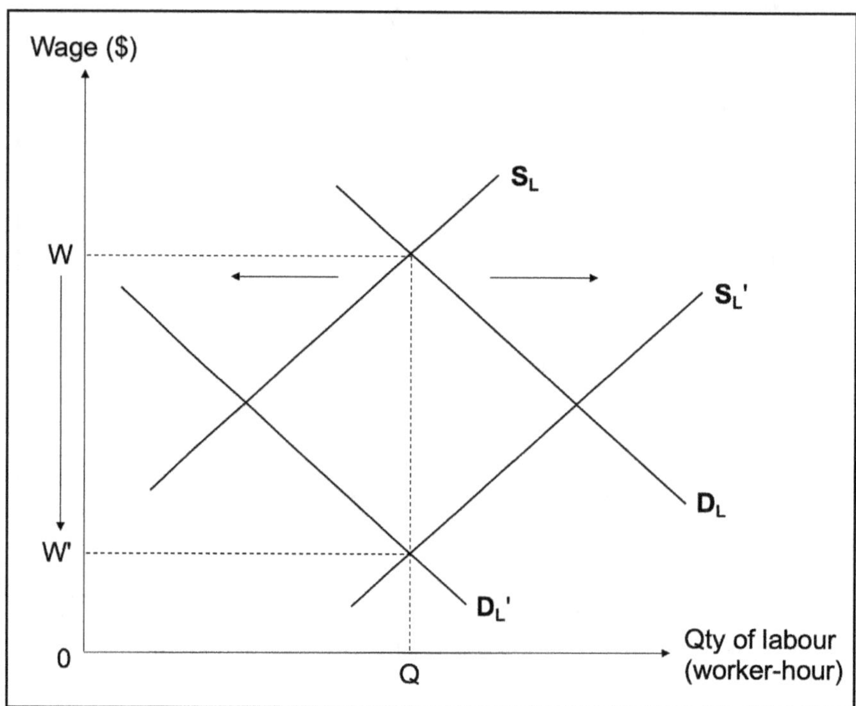

Fig. 18. The Market for Unskilled Labour.

<u>Conclusion</u>

1. With the wages of skilled labour increasing in tandem with the wages of unskilled labour decreasing, it is evident that this would translate to and thus account for the increasing income gap between skilled and unskilled workers in Singapore.

14. Is minimum wage the best policy to narrow the income gap in Singapore? (15)

Introduction

1. An income gap occurs when there is an inequitable distribution of income, and can be a result of a difference in skill levels for workers.

2. It can cause problems such as material hardship for lower income groups, and increased tension between the different income groups.

3. Hence, policies to narrow the income gap should be pursued if the income gap is deemed to be inequitable.

4. Various policies exist to address the income gap, including a minimum wage, progressive tax policy and transfer payments, as well as policies that deal with training and immigration of labour.

Minimum wage narrows the income gap in Singapore

1. An effective minimum wage is a legal wage established by the government above the market equilibrium wage for low-skilled labour.

2. It aims to narrow income gap by lifting the minimum wages earned by low-skilled labour.

3. A minimum wage policy can be effectively implemented as long as monitoring is carried out and enforcement actions are taken against errant employers.

4. Workers who are able to find jobs which pay minimum wage become better-off.

5. The income gap can be narrowed as it is the low-skilled workers, whose market-determined equilibrium wage was below minimum wage to begin with, who will be receiving increased income. In contrast, high-skilled workers are most likely already earning wages above the legal minimum wage, and would thus not be impacted by the minimum wage policy at all.

Minimum wage has limitations and leads to economic trade-offs

1. A minimum wage can cause an increase in the level of unemployment among unskilled workers.

2. Employers may cut back on the number of workers employed as these workers are now require higher wages.

3. While workers who are able to secure work will reap the benefits of the minimum wage, resulting in a closing of the income gap, there will also be some workers who are unable to find jobs that will become worse off.

4. In addition, a black market may occur where workers accept wages below equilibrium wage just to maintain or attain employment, which increases the income gap.

5. The combined effects of the minimum wage can be viewed below in Fig. 19.

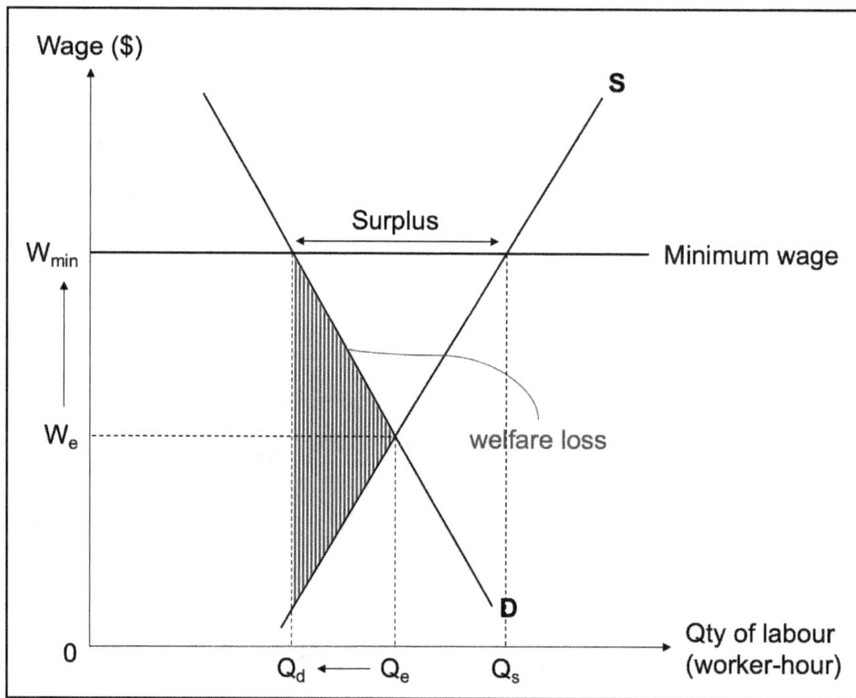

Fig. 19. An Analysis of the Consequences of implementing a Minimum Wage.

6. Referring to Fig. 19, the minimum wage is set at W_{min} above W_e, the market equilibrium level. Quantity of labour demanded is at Q_d and quantity of labour supplied is higher at Q_s.

7. Following the implementation of the minimum wage, Q_d number of workers are able to enjoy the higher wage of We. However, this comes at the expense of (Q_e – Q_d) workers being retrenched. Meanwhile, (Q_s – Q_e) number of workers, attracted by the higher wage W_{min}, now become willing and able to work and start actively seeking for employment — but they are now unable to find a job.

8. Similarly, the surplus of (Q_s – Q_d) workers may lead to the creation of a black market for labour, in which certain workers may be willing to work illegally to maintain employment, even at wage levels below W_{min} or W_e.

9. Such workers would be worse off, not only receiving a reduced wage, but also possibly facing unsafe working conditions or having their overtime work go uncompensated — a side effect of such black market jobs operating outside the purview of prevailing government legislation intended to safeguard workers.

10. These negative consequences are illustrated through the net Welfare Loss, indicated by the shaded area in Fig. 19.

11. In addition, the minimum wage can cause wage-push inflation, resulting in a tradeoff with other macroeconomic objectives.

12. This can result in an overall loss of competitiveness in the Singaporean economy as its goods and services become more expensive relative to trade competitors, which might lead to further retrenchment and increased unemployment, increasing the income gap.

13. Wage-push inflation could also cause a rise in the prices of daily necessities, placing a larger financial burden on low-income households, especially those retrenched or unable to find a job as a result of the minimum wage.

<u>A more progressive income tax system might be more effective in reducing the after-tax income gap</u>

1. A progressive income tax system occurs when people of different income levels are mandated to pay increasing taxes as their income increases.

2. To increase the progressivity of Singapore's income tax system, the proportion of taxes paid by higher income earners should be increased.

3. For instance, the highest marginal tax rate of 20% (for individuals earning more than S$ 320,000) could be increased.

4. This would reduce the after-tax income of higher income earners and hence reduce the after-tax income gap.

5. Moreover, the increase in tax revenue raised can be used to finance transfers to lower income earners.

6. However, limitations to the policy exist. Higher tax rates disincentivise work efforts, as the decreasing monetary reward for work may cause such high-income workers to choose to spend more of their time on leisure activities rather than work.

7. In addition, higher tax rates work against Singapore's persistent efforts in attracting global talents, which are essential to maintaining our comparative advantage, to relocate to Singapore.

<u>More targeted transfers from the government to low income earners will also reduce the income gap</u>

1. Transfer payments occur where the government gives out payments either through direct payments or vouchers to the lowest income members in society.

2. For example, under the Workfare Income Supplement scheme, low income earners are eligible for wage top-ups of up to S$ 700 per quarter from the government as long as they remain employed for at least 2 of 3 months. This can effectively increase the after-transfer income of low income earners, thus reducing the income gap.

3. Consequently, an increase in such payments would aid in further narrowing the income gap.

4. However, limitations of this policy do exist, and includes the high financial burden on the government of financing transfer payments.

5. Furthermore, low income workers and their employers may also become reliant on these transfer payments, and this may thus disincentivise them from improving their skills or productivity to seek out better-paying jobs to increase income.

Tightening of Singapore's unskilled foreign worker policy will reduce the income gap

1. A reduction in the number of employment passes issued to unskilled foreign workers will reduce the supply of unskilled labour.

2. As such, wages for unskilled labour will increase, ceteris paribus. This allows low income earners to earn higher wages resulting in a reduction in the income gap.

3. Alternatively, an increase in the foreign worker levy may be put in place, making unskilled foreign labour more expensive to hire. This will cause an increase in the demand for local unskilled workers as a substitute, resulting in higher wages and a reduction in the income gap.

4. However, there are several limitations to this policy. Firstly, this will likely drive up wage-push inflation, leading to significant micro and macroeconomic impacts as explained earlier.

5. Some jobs may also be unfilled as locals may shun jobs in certain labour-intensive industries such as construction or shipbuilding, in which unskilled foreign workers have typically constituted an overwhelming majority of the workforce, and as such these key industries may face a shortage of workers.

Skills upgrading policies will reduce the income gap

1. The government can also invest in policies aimed at training and education to allow unskilled workers to progress towards jobs that require more skilled labour, thusly allowing them to earn increased wages.

2. For example, under the Workfare Training Support Scheme, the Singapore government subsidises employers up to 95% of fees incurred in sending low income earners for approved training courses. The workers are also provided cash incentives for completing such courses.

3. Referring to Fig. 20 on the next page, workers that undergo such courses will be more skilled and productive, and as such will receive higher demand for their services at D_L', enabling more workers at Q_2 to be employed at higher wages of W_2.

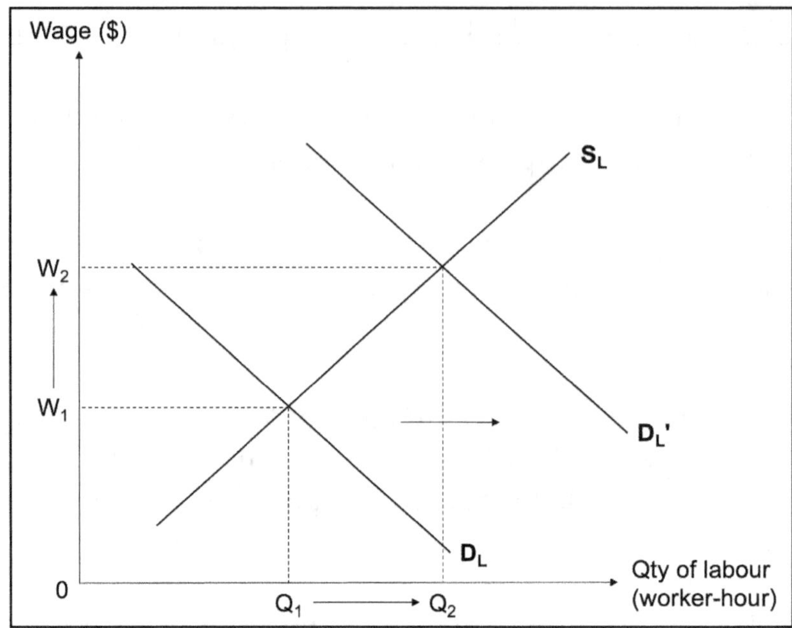

Fig. 20. Skills-upgrading courses leading to Increased Wages.

4. However, this policy also places a high burden on government finances, and may not achieve the desired results as the success of such skills-upgrading courses is heavily dependent upon the quality of courses as well as the receptiveness and capabilities of workers themselves.

5. In addition, the policy has time lags as it takes a significant time period to train and educate workers.

Concluding Section

1. While the minimum wage can be an effective tool in reducing the income gap, it comes with many undesirable side effects that may actually make the income gap worse, and is hence not the best policy in this situation.

2. Ideally, the competitiveness and vibrancy of the Singpaore economy should not be comprised in the attempt to close the income gap, and as such levelling up lower-skilled labour is preferred.

3. However, in the short term, a well calibrated increase in taxes combined with transfer payments can allow for an effective stopgap solution.

4. At the same time, skills upgrading policies are preferred in the long term as they can effectively address the root causes of the income gap issue, based on the disparity in skill levels.

15. Would you support the implication of this statement that inflation is caused by consumer spending? (15)

Introduction

1. Inflation is defined as a persistent increase in the General Price Level of the economy.

2. Inflation can be caused both by demand factors (demand pull inflation) and supply factors (cost push inflation).

Thesis: Higher Retail Spending can cause Inflation

1. Higher retail spending may imply higher domestic consumer spending, a component of aggregate demand, ceteris paribus.

2. The increase in consumption can trigger unplanned disinvestment for producers, in turn causing an increase in production in the next production cycle.

3. This increases demand for factor inputs that includes labour, leading to a subsequent increase in incomes for workers.

4. The rising incomes causes workers to have greater purchasing power, and leads to further spending after removing the amount spent on taxes, savings and imports.

5. This triggers multiple rounds of increases in aggregate demand, formed on the basis that one person's spending is another person's income that is further spent.

6. This process, known as the multiplier effect, repeats until the total withdrawals is equal to the initial increase in consumer spending.

7. With the multiplier process, an initial increase in consumer spending can lead to multiple rounds of aggregate demand increases.

8. As such, it is possible that an economy operating close to full capacity can experience demand pull inflation as a result of this.

9. This is as illustrated in Fig. 21 on the next page.

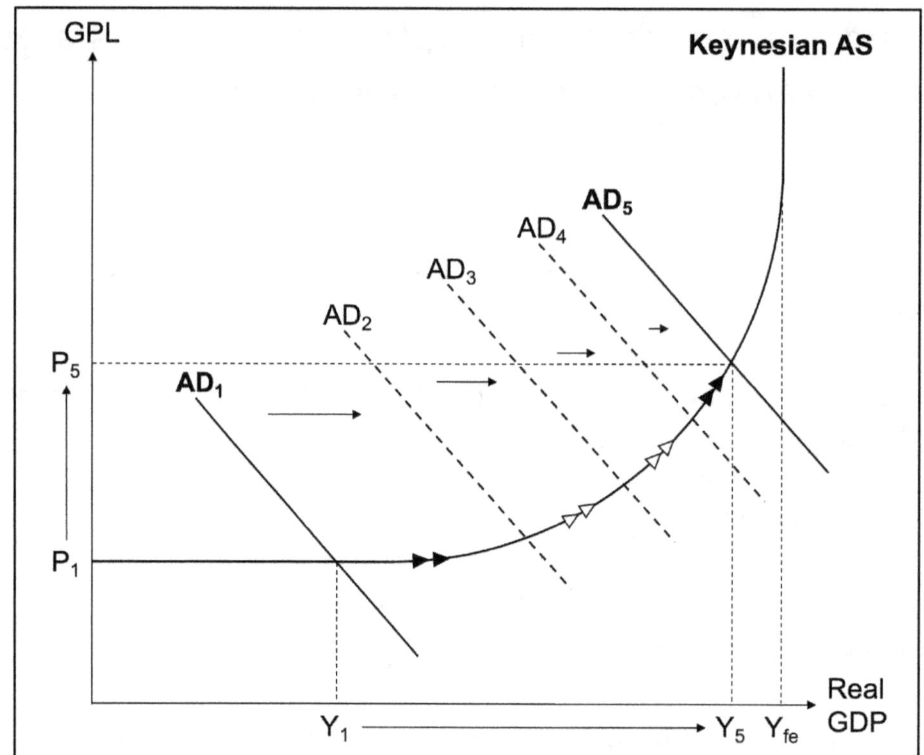

Fig. 21. Demand-Pull Inflation due to the Multiplier Effect.

10. As seen in Fig. 21, an initial autonomous increase in Consumer expenditure results in an increase in Aggregate Demand from AD_1 to AD_2. This then induces multiple rounds of subsequent increases through the multiplier effect, until AD finally increases to AD_5. In total, this results in General Price Levels rising significantly P_1 to P_5 as the economy expands and now operates at Y_5, very close to full capacity Y_{fe}.

<u>Anti-Thesis: Other Causes of Demand-Pull inflation exist</u>

1. However, the above is based on the ceteris paribus assumption, that may not hold true in real life.

2. Demand-pull inflation can also be caused by alternate factors besides consumer spending, such as government spending, investments or net exports.

3. G, I, and (X – M) are all components of aggregate demand, and can cause increases in aggregate demand as well as the multiplier effect.

4. As such, increases in G, I or (X – M) can also cause demand pull inflation, even if consumer spending remains relatively unchanged.

5. This is especially so for small and open economies such as Singapore, where economic growth is mainly reliant on external demand.

6. As such, with the small domestic market, consumer spending may be less of an influence on demand pull inflation as net exports, for example.

7. Consumer spending is hence not the only cause of demand-pull inflation.

Anti-Thesis: Inflation can also be caused by Cost-Push inflation

1. A rise in GPL can also be caused by cost-push inflation, which affects Aggregate Supply instead.

2. In the short run, this can be caused by an increase in prices for factors of production, which drives up the unit cost of production for goods in an economy. For instance, in 1973 there was a sharp rise in the price of oil, a factor input used in the production of virtually all goods and services in the economy, due to the OPEC oil embargo.

3. This led to a fall in the Short-Run Aggregate Supply from SRAS to SRAS', as illustrated in Fig. 22 below. In turn, this created a shortage at the original price level P, thereby placing inflationary pressures on the economy towards P'. This is just one instance of inflation occurring without any rises in consumer spending or AD.

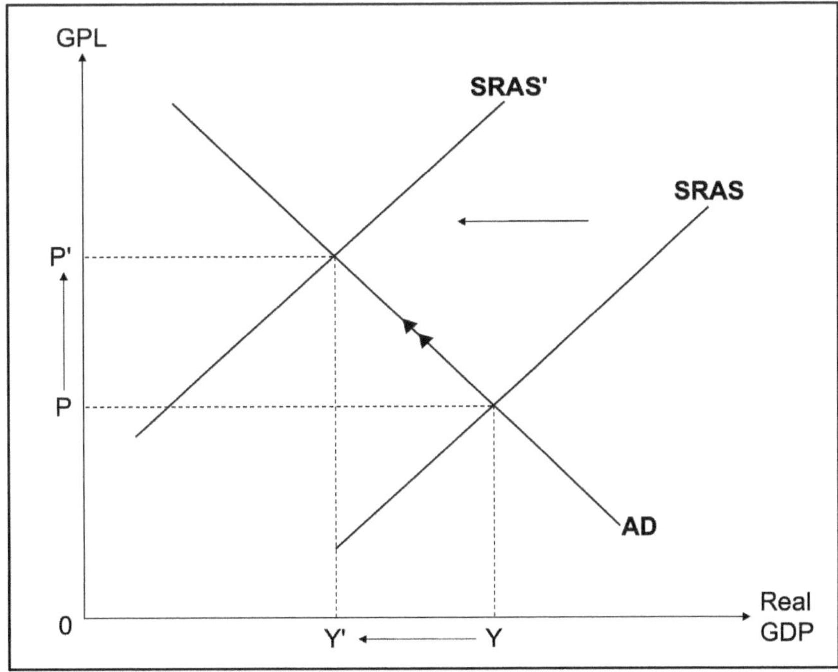

Fig. 22. Cost-Push Inflation as a result of a decrease in SRAS.

Concluding Section

1. There are many causes for inflation, both on demand pull and cost push sides.

2. Consumer spending can certainly be a cause for inflation.

3. However, consumer spending is not the only cause, and inflation is caused by a multitude of factors that impact both aggregate demand and aggregate supply.

16. Explain the effects of an increase in the level of investment by firms on output and prices in the economy. (10)

Introduction

1. Investments refer to spending by firms or the government in purchasing capital goods (machines, equipment, infrastructure, etc). They constitute a component of Aggregate Demand.

2. An increase in investments has both short and long term effects on the economy.

Short Term

1. An increase in investments will result in an increase in aggregate demand, ceteris paribus.

2. For instance, consider the scenario where $ 100 million of Investments are injected into circular flow of income.

3. This in turn creates a shortage. Firms deplete inventories (unplanned disinvestment), inducing firms to step up production in the next production cycle, increasing demand for factors of production that includes labour.

4. As such, employment of workers rises, who receive increased factor incomes.

5. However, households will not spend all of the increased income they receive, and would choose to save some of it, use it to pay taxes and spend some on imported goods — these are collectively known as withdrawals. As a result, the factor incomes earned and subsequently saved, paid as taxes and spent on imports would result in leakage out of the circular flow of income.

6. Assuming the Marginal Propensity to Withdraw is 0.6, these leakages would total $ 100 million x 0.6 = $ 60 million

7. On the other hand, the expenditure on domestic goods and services, which is caused by income induced consumption, will increase. This increase amounts to a total of $ 40 million, since the Marginal Propensity to Consume is 0.4, assuming MPC + MPW = 1.

8. The income-induced consumption (expenditure on domestic goods and services) of $ 40 million further creates a shortage again, causing firms to deplete inventories (unplanned disinvestment), and inducing firms to step up production in the next production cycle.

9. This further increases the employment of workers who receive more factor incomes and induces a subsequent round of expenditure on domestic goods and services totalling $ 16 million — assuming MPC remains constant at 0.4. This in turn causes firms to continue to expanding production, increasing real National Income by a further $ 16 million.

10. This cycle of induced consumption is the Keynesian Multiplier Effect, which works on the basis that one group's spending becomes another group's income, which further induces more spending and income.

11. The cycle repeats itself until the sum of initial injection = total withdrawal, which is $ 100 million.

12. The effects on output and prices will depend on the size of the multiplier and the state of the economy.

13. The multiplier size determines the amount of income that will be further spent on goods and services. A larger multiplier size will result in a larger overall increase in aggregate demand, potentially allowing the output of the economy to increase to a larger extent. This also causes firms to bid up prices on factor inputs including labour, causing an increase in the General Price Level across the economy.

14. However, this is still dependent on the state of the economy. An economy operating at or close to full capacity will not experience the full multiplier effect, as there may be a shortage of workers to fulfil the increased demand, leading to limited increases in output. At the same time, as factor inputs become increasingly scarce within the economy, prices begin to skyrocket, increasing exponentially compared to the growth in real output, leading to high levels of inflation

15. Conversely, if economy is operating well below full employment output level, the economy will be able to harness the full extent of the multiplier effect, allowing for large increases output. GPL will remain relatively stable, increasing in tandem with the growth in real output, allowing for low to moderate levels of inflation.

Long Run

1. An increase in investment typically causes an increase in productive capacity in the long run.

2. This is because increased investments result in capital accumulation in the long run, increasing the quantity and quality of factor inputs. For instance, should the previously-mentioned $ 100 million investment come in the form of road construction projects, this would increase the quantity and quality of existing transportation services, reducing the lost productive man-hours spent on transportation each and every day, hence allowing workers in the economy to be more productive.

3. This increases the productive capacity of the economy from Y_{fe} to Y_{fe}', illustrated through a rightward shift of the Keynesian Aggregate Supply curve in the long run as seen in Fig. 23 below.

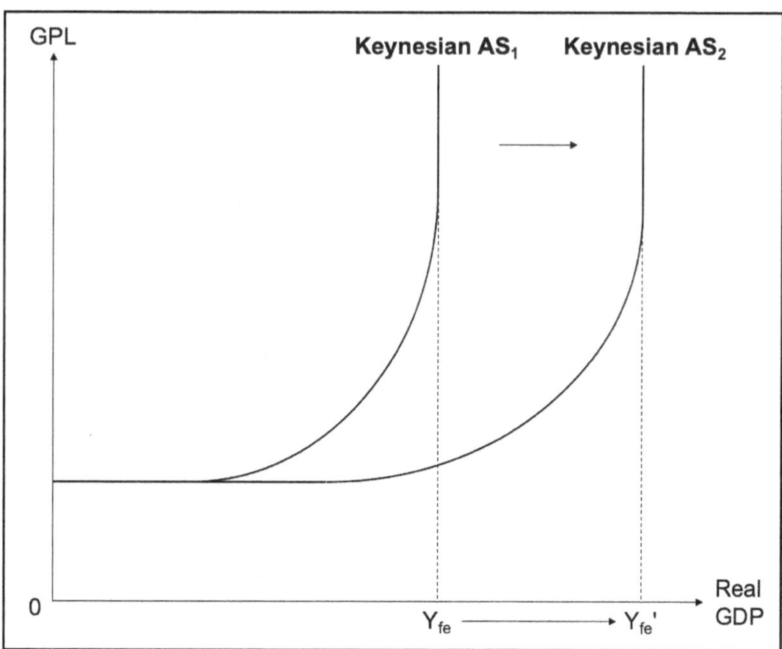

Fig. 23. Investments leading to an increase in AS.

4. An increased productive capacity would allow for aggregate demand to continue to grow with limited inflationary impacts, allowing the full multiplier effect to be enjoyed.

5. As such, real output will increase in the long run combined with a fall in prices as inflationary pressures are alleviated.

17. Discuss the possible impacts of a world-wide recession on Singapore. (15)

Introduction

1. A world-wide recession means that real national incomes are falling globally.

2. This can be triggered, for example, due to the COVID-19 pandemic that resulted in "lockdowns" and border closures across the world.

3. This led to major adverse demand shocks to industries such as air travel and tourism. The lockdowns resulted in a collapse of demand and production, which resulted in massive layoffs, falling incomes and further falls in consumption and investments world-wide.

4. This will have very significant impacts on Singapore, which can be analysed in terms of the key economic indicators - economic growth rates, unemployment rates, balance of payments (BOP) and inflation rates.

Negative impact on Current Account and Economic Growth

1. A world-wide recession will adversely affect Singapore's current account and capital account of the Balance of Payments.

2. As incomes of our trading partners fall, there will be a fall in demand for Singapore's exports, especially in major export commodities like chemicals and electronics. Thus, export revenues will fall.

3. However, given the reliance on imported necessities due to a lack of natural resources, import expenditure will not decrease by much. For example, Singapore will still continue to import oil, natural gas and agricultural produce.

4. This will lead to a significant worsening of the Balance of Trade, the most significant component of the Current Account, and thus the worsening of the Current Account as well.

5. Similarly, this decrease in export revenue will mean that the net exports component of Aggregate Demand (AD) will fall. Given the large dependence of the economy on exports for growth due to the small domestic market arising from a small population, the AD will likely fall from AD to AD′ as seen in Fig below and via the reverse multiplier process, the RGDP is likely to fall more than proportionately and the economy thus experiences a recession as seen in Fig 1.

6. This is further exacerbated by a fall in household and business confidence which would reduce the consumption and investment components of the AD, further reducing the AD.

7. As firms cut production, workers will be laid off and thus demand deficient unemployment increases as the economy moves further away from the full employment level of output Yfe.

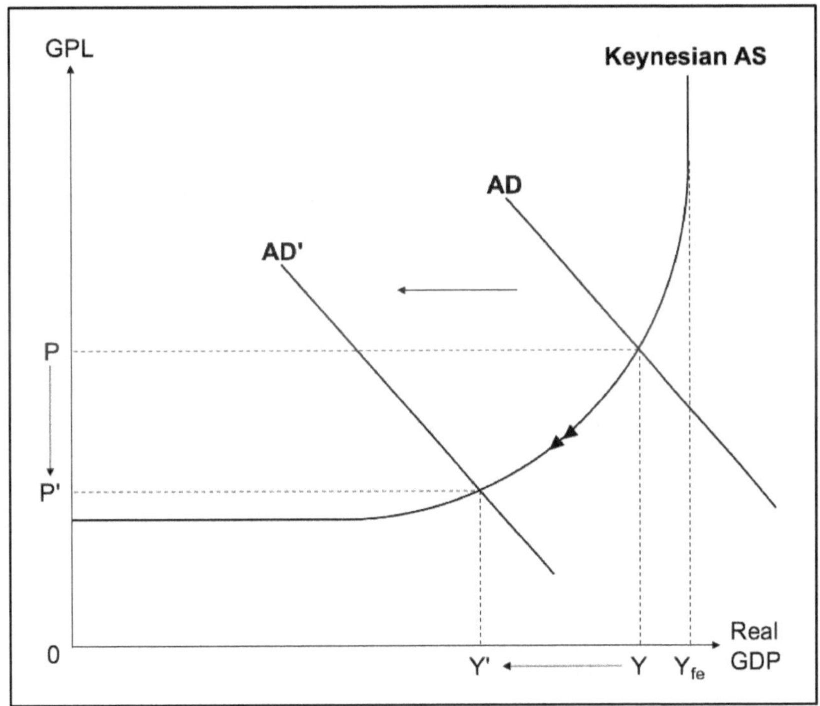

Fig. 24. Worldwide recession causing recession in Singapore

Negative Impact on Financial Account and BOP

1. In addition, given a world-wide fall in income, investors are likely to be more averse to investments as confidence in the world's and Singapore's economy would decrease.

2. Long term capital flow into Singapore will thus fall. Hence, the financial account is also likely to worsen.

3. With a worsening of both the current and financial account, overall BOP is likely to worsen sharply and Singapore may thus experience a BOP deficit.

Adverse Long-term Impact

1. Should the fall in investments including foreign direct investments into Singapore be prolonged, there would be serious adverse impacts on the potential economic growth rates and this long-term economic growth prospects.

2. This is because with a fall in investments, there will be a slowdown in capital accumulation. If the fall is drastic and prolonged, there may not even be enough new capital goods to replace worn out ones and the capital stock may thus shrink.

3. Similarly, workers who are retrenched for extended periods of time during the recession may face a 'de-skilling' process, rendering them less productive. Some retrenched workers, unable to find a job and disillusioned with the job search process, may even lose motivation to the extent of giving up on employment altogether, effectively dropping out of the labour force.

4. Consequently, the quantity and quality of existing factors of production within the Singapore economy may decrease, leading to a reduction in our productive capacity and long-term economic growth prospects.

Positive Impact on Investments and Financial Account

1. However, it could also be argued that a global recession would, in fact, increase the levels of investment in the Singapore economy.

2. It is pertinent to note that the global recession would dampen business outlooks in every economy — not just Singapore's. Therefore, the question comes down to which economy is best positioned to weather the prevailing economic headwinds.

3. The Singapore economy, with its high degree of political stability reputation for sound social and economic policies, stable exchange rate, large Forex and

national reserves might thus prove to be an attractive prospect to investors, in comparison with many other economies that might be in a more precarious position.

4. For this reason, foreign direct investment inflows and portfolio investment inflows may increase and the financial account may improve instead.

5. The increased investments could also serve as a stimulus to the Singapore economy, reducing the recessionary impact on real output and unemployment. The direct investments could also sustain potential economic growth and thus long term growth prospects.

Positive Impact on BOT / BOP and Price Stability

1. During a global recession, with production activities worldwide grinding to a halt, the demand for factor inputs and commodities (such as oil) would fall, translating to a fall in their prices as well.

2. Since Singapore is highly reliant on imported factor inputs to manufacture value-added goods, the fall in commodity prices would reduce the cost of production.

3. The Short-Run Aggregate Supply increases, mitigating the fall in output and employment explained earlier. It also reduces the GPL as shown in Fig 25, contributing to a lower rate of inflation.

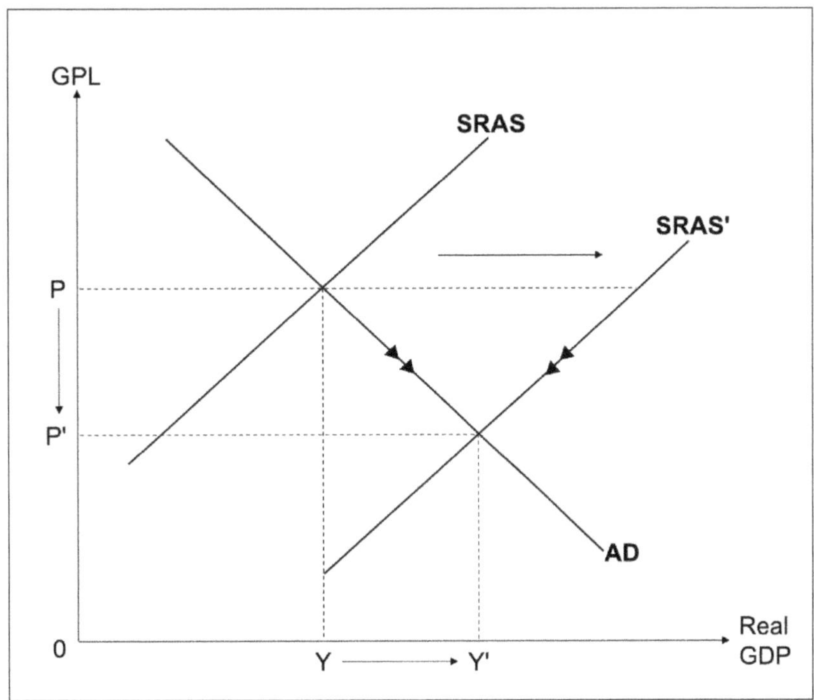

Fig. 25. Effect of an increase in the SRAS

4. With a fall in the GPL, this allows Singapore's exports to be more price competitive, most likely mitigating the loss in export revenue due to falling incomes.

5. Additionally, with falling prices of imported inputs, Singapore's import expenditure would decrease as her demand for imports is expected to be price-inelastic due to a lack of domestic substitutes available, leading to a less than proportionate increase in imports.

6. Therefore, the BOT may not necessarily worsen and should capital inflows increase, the BOP may not worsen as previously explained and may in fact improve.

7. However, it should also be noted that there could be a danger of deflation since both the fall in AD and an increase in the SRAS, lowers the GPL. This can spark off deflationary spirals, where C and I continue to fall due to the deflation, leading to further falls in AD and GPL leading to a vicious downward spiral of falling price levels, output and employment.

Concluding Section

1. Due to Singapore's small and open economy, the impacts of a worldwide recession would hit exceptionally hard. This stems from the reliance of the Singapore economy on the outlook of the global economy. As such, with a negative global outlook, the Singaporean economy would face relatively severe negative impacts, especially in terms of recession and unemployment.

2. However, there are mitigating factors as discussed. In addition, the Singapore Government is known to be capable of found macroeconomic policies and would likely allow the S$ to depreciate as well as implement a slew of fiscal and supply-side policies. This is aided by the strong financial capability of the Government due to years of accumulated budget surpluses.

3. Much would depend on how prolonged the worldwide recession is. During the global recession sparked off by the US financial crisis in 2009, many economies rebounded quite quickly and the Singapore economy likewise rebounded along rapidly. This may not be in the case of the COVID-19 pandemic.

18. Explain the factors affecting the level of investments in your country. (10)

Introduction

1. Investment is the act of acquiring new fixed capital assets (e.g. new plants, new machinery) and accumulating physical stocks and inventories (e.g. raw materials, semi-finished goods and finished goods held by the producer).

2. An investment project can be considered profitable if the expected rate of return (Exp RoR) on a project is higher than or equal to interest rates (cost of funds).

Expected Rates of Return

1. The level of investment in an economy is jointly determined by the Exp RoR on various investment projects and interest rates.

2. The Exp RoR varies according to factors such as the level of business confidence.

3. However, since the Exp RoR only gives information about the potential benefits of an investment project, it is only one part of the decision making equation for investments.

Interest Rates

1. Potential investors also need to pay an interest rate for the finance borrowed. This denotes the cost of financing the investment project.

2. The higher the interest rate, the higher the cost and hence the more expensive it will be for firms to finance investment projects.

3. As a result, fewer investment projects are profitable, thereby reducing investment levels in the economy.

4. When interest rates rise, the opportunity cost of using internal funds to finance investment projects also rises. This is because some investment projects may not take place if firms decide that they can attain a better rate of return by depositing funds into a bank.

5. As seen in Fig. 26 below, an increase in the interest rate would denote a shift along the Demand for Investments curve (DDI), thereby leading to a decreased quantity of investment conducted as fewer investment projects are profitable.

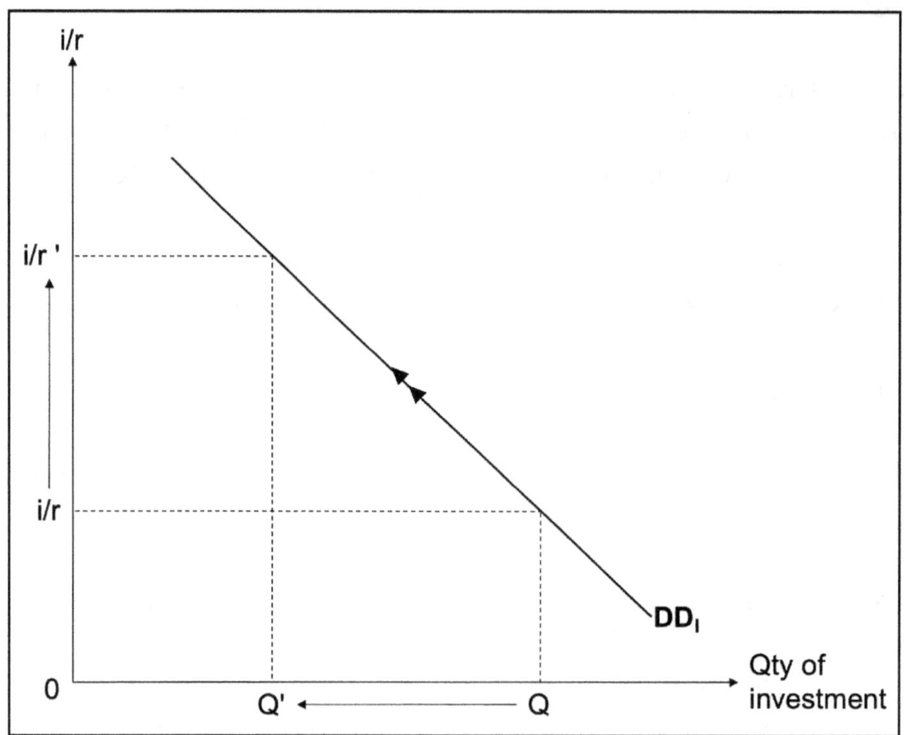

Fig. 26. Effect of an increase in interest rates on the quantity of investment.

6. The converse is true and investment increases when interest rate decreases.

Determinants of Exp RoR

7. The Exp RoR depends on several factors such as business confidence, political stability, the quality of infrastructure, government policies, the quality of workforce and good labour management relationship.

8. If business sentiments improve, firms would expect to yield greater future/ potential profits and income streams from any investment projects they are considering.

9. Hence when businessmen are optimistic about the demand for their goods and the prospects of making profits, investments increase. The converse is however also true, where a loss of business confidence would decrease investments as the expectations of returns on investments fall.

10. Good infrastructure such as effective transport and communications networks together with a strong and efficient government encourages investment to take place. The economy would be able to run at higher productivity levels as a direct result of the lower costs of production brought about by better infrastructure. Thus, expected rate of return on investment projects increases and investment expenditure increases.

11. Singapore, in particular, has the advantage in having a politically stable environment as she is renowned for her sound governance with political continuity and effective law enforcement, especially on control of corruption. As a result of such qualitative factors, firms are more inclined to conduct investments in Singapore, with the assurance and peace-of-mind that their investment projects come with decreased risks.

12. Additionally, policies by the Singapore government have created an economic environment that invites investment by firms. Such policies are implemented on the basis of supporting and increasing the after-tax incomes of firms, allowing them to have greater incentive and ability to conduct investments.

13. For example, a reduction in corporate tax will increase after-tax profits and hence the rate of return on investment. Thus, investment levels would increase. In Singapore, government policies of granting generous tax deductions for accelerated development and tax holidays for pioneer companies have a tendency to stimulate investment.

14. When the literacy rate of a country improves, it can result in a workforce which is easier to train, more receptive to changes, and is more productive.

15. This reduces labour costs incurred by firms, thereby reducing the cost of production, and allowing for greater expected rates of return on investment projects.

16. Such labour productivity can be increased through various skills training programmes, which Singapore has an abundance of.

17. For instance, employers in Singapore can send their workers for retraining and skills upgrades, often at a hefty government subsidy.

18. Singapore also has a harmonious tripartite relationship between the government, unions, and employers. This keeps in check potential issues with regard to repeated increases in wages and also prevents wage spirals. This keeps labour

costs low for potential investors, increasing the Exp RoR on investment projects and hence increasing investment.

19. This is supported by the easy access to a talented workforce as Singapore also adopts an open-door policy for international talents and expertise, further enhancing the quality of its workforce.

20. Decreased labour costs and increased business confidence lead firms to forecast greater Exp RoR ob investment projects at all levels of interest rates. This is diagrammatically illustrated, in Fig. 27, as a rightward shift of the Demand for Investments curve from DD_I to DD_I'. At each and every interest rate i/r, the quantity of investment has increased.

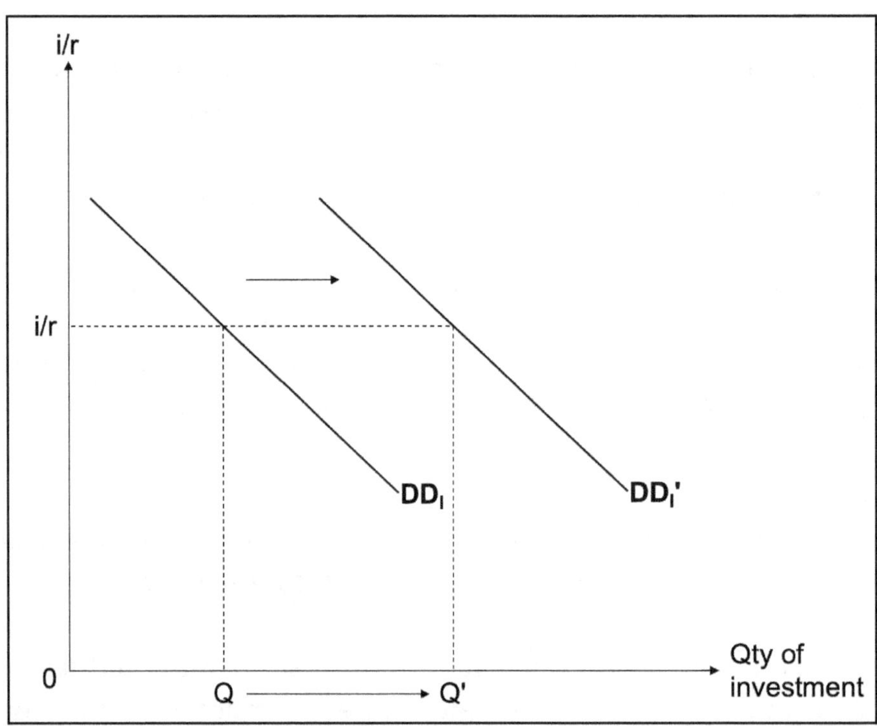

Fig. 27. Effect of decreased labour costs on the quantity of investment.

19. Discuss the extent to which the size of Singapore's national income multiplier would affect the effectiveness of her macroeconomic policies. (15)

Introduction

1. Singapore is a small and open economy, with a lack of resources, and high Marginal Propensity to Import (MPM) and Marginal Propensity to Save (MPS).

2. As such, the value of the national income Keynesian multiplier in Singapore is likely to be relatively low compared to other countries.

3. The government has undertaken a few policies to manage the Singapore economy.

4. Firstly, the government has pursued a Gradual and Modest Appreciation exchange rate policy to curb imported cost-push inflation while balancing export competitiveness and demand-pull inflation arising from strong external demand.

5. Secondly, the government has enacted Fiscal policy alongside strong Supply-Side policies to increase productive capacity of the economy and boost international competitiveness.

6. Thirdly, the government has implemented trade policies to expand trade network continuously and reduce barriers of trade.

Thesis: A small multiplier can limit the effectiveness of Singapore's Demand-side policies

1. A small Keynesian multiplier value implies that little income is passed on within the circular flow of income to induce subsequent rounds of spending and income gains.

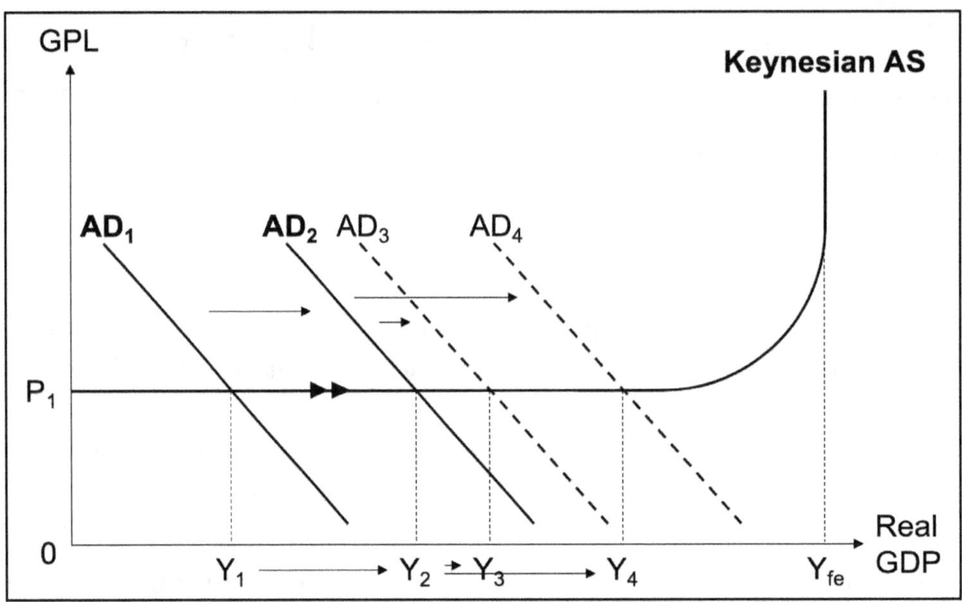

Fig. 28. Illustrating the difference between a Small and a Large Keynesian Multiplier.

2. As is illustrated in Fig. 28, should the Keynesian multiplier value be of a large magnitude, the initial increase in AD (from AD_1 to AD_2) would induce a great amount of subsequent spending (AD_2 to AD_4). This is in contrast to economies with a smaller multiplier value, wherein the induced subsequent spending would be significantly smaller (AD_2 to AD_3).

3. Thus, the overall growth rate with a large multiplier value (Y_1 to Y_4) is significantly greater than it would be with a smaller multiplier value (Y_1 to Y_3). Hence, it is evident that a smaller multiplier value causes a slower economic growth rate.

4. As such, demand management policies like an expansionary monetary policy (whether through fiscal or monetary means) will result in Singapore experiencing smaller successive increases in aggregate demand, and thus a reduced overall increase in Aggregate Demand.

5. This will hamper the effectiveness of demand management policies as a primary driver of economic growth, as more initial injection into the economy is needed to achieve the same amount of economic growth as an economy with a larger multiplier size.

6. As such, the smaller multiplier size calls the need for greater intervention, and also requires the government to be more focused and selective in its fiscal policy.

7. In addition, due to Singapore's small nature and reliance on imported goods, it is unable to rely too extensively on exchange rate policy as a means to drive Aggregate Demand growth. Although a weakened exchange rate is able to increase exports, it would make Singapore susceptible to imported inflation, as imported goods become relatively more expensive in terms of the weakened Singapore dollar. Hence, it is evident that government responses to a small multiplier value are also limited.

<u>Anti-Thesis: Singapore's reliance on supply side policies and trade policies would mean that the multiplier would have limited impact</u>

1. As Singapore is a small economy with limited resources, there is a need to increase its productive capacity continuously.

2. Consequently, the majority of the Singapore government's Fiscal policies are also implemented with Supply-Side slants in mind, such as accelerating the construction of key infrastructure like roads as well as industrial and technological hubs. This is in addition to dedicated Supply-Side Policies aimed at increasing productivity. Such policies serve to increase the quantity and quality of Factors of Production.

3. Supply-Side policies work through increasing Aggregate Supply, and do not directly affect Aggregate Demand, hence such policies are able to circumvent the limitations imposed by a small multiplier value.

4. Additionally, as a country with a small population, Singapore also faces the problem of having a small domestic demand, hence it is dependent on external trade to drive increases in AD and economic growth.

5. As such, the Singapore government has placed much focus and emphasis on its pursuit of trade policies, mainly involving the creation/expansion of Free Trade Agreements to expand its trade network, and to reduce/remove trade barriers. Such trade policies are also not dependent on the size of the multiplier.

6. Given the nature of Singapore's economy, supply side policies and trade policies are likely to remain as institutional economic policies, where its effectiveness would not be directly affected by the small multiplier size.

Anti-Thesis: Other limitations to Singapore's economy are more significant than the size of Singapore's multiplier

1. Firstly, due to Singapore's small economy, 'hot money' flows form a large part of the capital base, and as such interest rates are difficult to maintain and control.

2. Consequently, Singapore is a price taker in terms of interest rates.

3. This limits the number of policy instruments the government can take in managing the economy — its central bank cannot rely upon quantitative easing and other interest-rate-oriented policy solutions to achieve its various macroeconomic objectives.

4. Secondly, Singapore is extremely vulnerable to changes in business confidence as part of the global economic climate.

5. This stems from the openness of the Singaporean economy: its reliance on Foreign Domestic Investment and external demand for growth in place of the smaller domestic economy.

6. Hence Singapore's economic performance is extremely dependent on the global economic performance as a whole. In times of an international economic downturn, there is little the government can do to unilaterally lift the Singapore economy out of the recession, and much of its efforts would instead focus on mere amelioration.

7. Thirdly, Singapore could potentially face increasing budget difficulties, especially in the light of an ageing population, that may require increased government spending on healthcare and other welfare items.

8. As such, embarking on high-budget expansionary fiscal policies may thus become increasingly difficult for the government.

9. Lastly, the Singapore government faces a difficult balancing act in terms of managing conflicts between its macroeconomic goals.

10. On one hand, Singapore pursues a gradual and modest appreciation of the Singapore dollar to fight against imported cost-push inflation and demand pull inflation.

11. However, this appreciation may harm its economic competitiveness, as the price of Singaporean exports in terms of foreign currencies would become relatively more expensive. This would, in turn, hamper export revenue and economic growth, especially since Singapore is extremely dependent on external demand for growth.

12. Therefore the government needs to be constantly proactive in balancing between the need for export-driven economic growth, and the need to guard against imported cost-push inflation.

13. The above-mentioned four issues, especially in combination, constitute a far greater concern affecting the effectiveness of Singapore's macroeconomic policies. In comparison, a small multiplier value may be the least of Singapore's concerns.

Concluding Section

1. It is true that the smaller multiplier size will limit the effectiveness of demand management policies in Singapore.

2. However, this does not apply to all policies.

3. Given Singapore's existing policy focus on improving its productive capacity and international competitiveness (in light of the small and open nature of its economy), a small multiplier size is a relatively less important concern. There are more severe problems and limitations affecting the Singapore economy, which the government has to keep in mind when crafting its policies.

20. Explain why the value of the national income multiplier might differ between countries. (10)

Introduction

1. The Keynesian multiplier provides a numerical value or estimate of an expected increase in income per dollar injected into the economy.

2. The size of the multiplier is determined by the Marginal Propensity to Withdraw, where the multiplier value (k) is given by —

$$k = \frac{1}{MPW}$$

3. The marginal propensity to withdraw is the sum of the Marginal Propensity to Save, Tax and Import (MPS, MPT and MPM, respectively).

4. Since the value of the multiplier is inversely proportional to MPW, the larger the MPW, the smaller the multiplier will be. So the higher the propensity to save, tax or import, the less that is passed on through the circular flow of income, and the lower the value of the multiplier will be.

5. The value of the multiplier differs between countries, since each country has a different value of MPS, MPT and MPM, and together this means that every country's MPW is different, therefore the multiplier value will also vary between countries..

MPM differs between countries

1. Countries that have smaller and more open economies would have larger MPMs.

2. This stems from the small factor endowment enjoyed by such countries, which makes it necessary to import a lot of raw materials to meet demand from the export market.

3. These countries also need to import most of their final goods and services to meet demand from demand from domestic market, for instance food products.

4. Larger economies on the other hand may be more self-sufficient in terms of factor endowment and would require fewer imports, and as such can afford to be less open than smaller economies.

5. For instance, Singapore (as a small and open economy) would have a relatively larger MPM value than that of other larger and less open countries such as Brazil, which imports the least amount of goods measured as a percentage of its GDP.

6. In addition, higher rates of economic growth and higher per capita income in some countries (relative to others) can also encourage imports.

7. The higher the level of national income, the greater the purchasing power of consumers. This increases the ability to purchase imported goods and services, which could be deemed as "higher quality" or may hold a certain brand appeal.

8. This causes a rise in MPM and hence a reduction in the multiplier.

MPT also differs between countries

1. Different countries have different tax systems, that can also influence the size of the multiplier.

2. A country with high government expenditure would need to impose higher tax rates in order to finance their expenditure. This country that has higher tax rates may thus have a smaller multiplier compared to other countries.

3. Most of the world's highest tax rates can be found in Western European countries, due to their comprehensive social safety network that entails high amounts of government expenditure on welfare programmes.

4. In Singapore, MPT has been declining over time. This is because the government had been decreasing the personal income and corporate tax rates in recent years in order to maintain international competitiveness, and as such MPT has been falling.

MPS also differs between countries

1. Asian countries tend to have a higher MPS compared to other countries.

2. This may be partly due to a cultural factor that includes a culture of thriftiness as compared to a culture of consumerism in Western societies.

3. In Asian countries, the increased propensity to save voluntarily for retirement or for medical expenditures may also stem from a lack of established social safety networks.

4. A widening income gap, especially between skilled and unskilled workers, may also prompt a higher MPS. This is because with an unequal income distribution, the national income will tend to accumulate in the hands of the rich, rather than the poor. With the rich having satisfied most of their basic wants, they will then tend to save more of any additional increase in their income. This unequal distribution of income hence prompts an increase in MPS driven primarily by higher income earners.

5. With regard to Singapore specifically, Singapore's unique CPF scheme also results in a higher MPS. Singapore has one of the highest savings rate in the world, and this is largely attributed to a forced savings policy by the government, whereby a portion of the monthly income of Singaporean workers is placed into the Central Provident Fund.

<u>Conclusion</u>

1. Thus, the MPM, MPT and MPS of different countries differ due to the difference in their economies.

2. In general, the size of the multiplier tends to be greater in economies that are big and less open, and lesser in small and more open economies.

3. Given the relatively large MPM and MPS of Singapore, the value of the national income multiplier in Singapore is likely to be relatively low compared to other countries.

www.ingramcontent.com/pod-product-compliance
Lightning Source LLC
LaVergne TN
LVHW061253100826
845148LV00008B/1108